STONEWORK
FOR THE GARDEN

STONEWORK
FOR THE GARDEN
Including 16 easy-to-build projects

ALAN & GILL BRIDGEWATER

NH
NEW
HOLLAND

This paperback edition first published in 2008 by
New Holland Publishers (UK) Ltd

London • Cape Town • Sydney • Auckland

24 Nutford Place, London WIH 6DQ, United Kingdom

80 McKenzie Street, Cape Town, 8001, South Africa

Unit 1, 66 Gibbes Street, Chatswood, NSW 2067, Australia

Unit IA, 218 Lake Road, Northcote, Auckland

10 9 8 7 6 5 4 3 2 1

ISBN 978 1 84773 169 2

Editorial Direction: Rosemary Wilkinson
Project Editor: Kate Latham
Production: Caroline Hansell

Designed and created for New Holland by AG&G BOOKS
Design: Glyn Bridgewater
Illustrators: Alan and Gill Bridgewater
Project design: Alan and Gill Bridgewater
Photography: Ian Parsons
Editor: Fiona Corbridge
Stonework: Alan and Gill Bridgewater

Reproduction by Modern Age Repro House Ltd, Hong Kong
Printed and bound in Malaysia by Times Offset (M) Sdn. Bhd.

Contents

Part 1: Techniques *8*

Part 2: Projects *32*

Introduction

When we first saw the stone walls that formed the garden boundary of our Cornish quayside cottage, we were amazed. They were beautiful! Ranging in height from a metre to well over three metres, the walls were massively thick and built from course upon course of uncut limestone. And so it was with all the walls in the village. We were brought to a standstill not only by the sheer size of the structures, but also by their physical presence and the fact that every single stone was set in place without mortar.

From then on, we were hooked. We began to scour the countryside for examples of interesting stonework. Over the next few years, we saw stone steps that disappeared into the sea, massive stonework railway arches built by Isambard Kingdom Brunel, tin mine towers, stone cellars, and so on. After years of looking and touching, exploring and drawing, we wanted to have a go at stonework ourselves. We began to search for some good "how-to" books, but soon discovered that although there were plenty of books that described stone structures, there was nothing much that actually told you how to mix the mortar and set one stone upon another. We came to the conclusion that if we wanted to do

stonework, we simply had to get on with it. As a result, we have worked on all manner of garden stonework projects – everything from walls and pillars, paths and rockeries, through to Japanese gardens and gateposts – and enjoyed it immensely.

Stonework is an amazingly vigorous and dynamic craft. The forms are large and bold, the techniques are adventurous and expressive, and the end results are truly monumental and last forever. We invite you to roll up your sleeves, take up the challenge, and build something that you will be very proud of!

Alan& Gill

Part I: Techniques

Designing and planning

The secret of building a successful stonework feature lies in the detail. It does not matter whether you are young or old, what is more important is enthusiasm and a willingness to spend time designing and planning the whole operation – from choosing the individual stones, through to organizing the delivery, mixing the mortar, and cleaning your tools. Stonework will enhance any garden, whether it is large or small.

FIRST CONSIDERATIONS

- Do you live in an area where the predominant building material is stone? Are there stone quarries within a radius of 20 kilometres?
- If most of the houses near you are built from brick and wood (therefore the chances are that there are no stone quarries in your area), are there any other sources of supply, such as builder's merchants or architectural salvage companies?
- Will local companies deliver small quantities of mixed stone?
- Is there adequate access to your garden – a road clear of traffic, a wide gateway, and a good drive?
- If the stone is unloaded in your driveway, or at your gate, will it cause any problems of access for you or your car? Will it damage the surface of the drive? Will it pose a danger to children or passers-by?
- How are you going to move the stone from the gate to the site? Are you going to move it yourself with a wheelbarrow and a sack barrow? Or are you going to ask friends to help, then move it with the aid of levers and rollers?
- Is your garden reasonably level, with paths wide enough for a wheelbarrow? Or does it have a lot of lawn and few pathways – if so, how will you move the materials?

Choosing a suitable project

When you have found satisfactory solutions to sourcing the stone and have worked out how and when it is going to be delivered, you can start to consider the ergonomics of the projects in the context of your specific needs: this boils down to working out how you are going to move the stone around the garden. In most instances, we have specifically designed the projects so that they are made up from small, easy-to-lift stones (albeit the sum total weight of all the stones might be considerable), but one or two of the projects do use single, monolithic stones. For example, if you have chosen to make the Pedestal Table (page 120), you have to work out how you are going to lift the table slab into position. There are a couple of ways to deal with it: you can build the pedestal before you take delivery of the table slab, then ask the stone supplier to lift the slab straight into position, or you can call on your friends and family to help you. The only thing you mustn't do is back down from building the project!

Planning the project

Whoever said that stonework is made up in equal parts of inspiration, perspiration, and planning, was right. Miscalculations can result in many hours of wasted time and effort. For example, when we failed to remember that a three-tonne delivery of gravel was arriving one day, it was simply tipped in our gateway. It was a good thing the sun was shining, because we spent about eighteen hours moving it in a wheelbarrow – just so we could use the car!

Plan your projects in as much detail as possible. It makes sense to schedule the building for a time of year when the weather is likely to be reasonable, so that the concrete will dry quickly and easily, and does not need to be protected from frost. When you have taken delivery of the sand, cement and stone, you need to consider the finer points of the operation. Is the structure going to get in the way of other activities? Is the ground so boggy, bumpy or rocky that you need to rethink the foundation? Are you building over an existing underground electricity cable? Is the structure going to cause water to collect? Are all the comings and goings with wheelbarrow and water going to damage the lawn? Are neighbours going to object? And so on. When all these questions have been answered, move all the materials to the site and cover them so that they are shielded from the weather.

Buying the right tools and materials

When you are starting to do stonework, buy yourself a basic, inexpensive tool kit appropriate for the project that you intend to make. But in the long run, expensive, high-quality tools are the best option, because they will last for years.

It is sensible for beginners to buy their materials one bag at a time; however, it is far cheaper to order sand, gravel, cement and rock in bulk. For example, twenty 50 kg bags of gravel purchased one at a time from the local builder's merchant cost the same as a 4-tonne lorry-load of loose gravel ordered from a quarry. Much the same goes for all the other materials. So, buy materials in bulk if possible to cut costs to the minimum.

The general rule of thumb is the more you want to buy, the lower the cost per unit, and most specialist suppliers are more than happy to haggle over the price. So, phone up at least three suppliers, specify your needs, and see who gives you the lowest quote. Then ask the other two suppliers if they want to better that price. Once you have agreed the price over the phone, ask the supplier to confirm your order in writing, setting out the product quantities, the total cost, and the delivery date and time.

STONEWORK DESIGNS FOR THE GARDEN

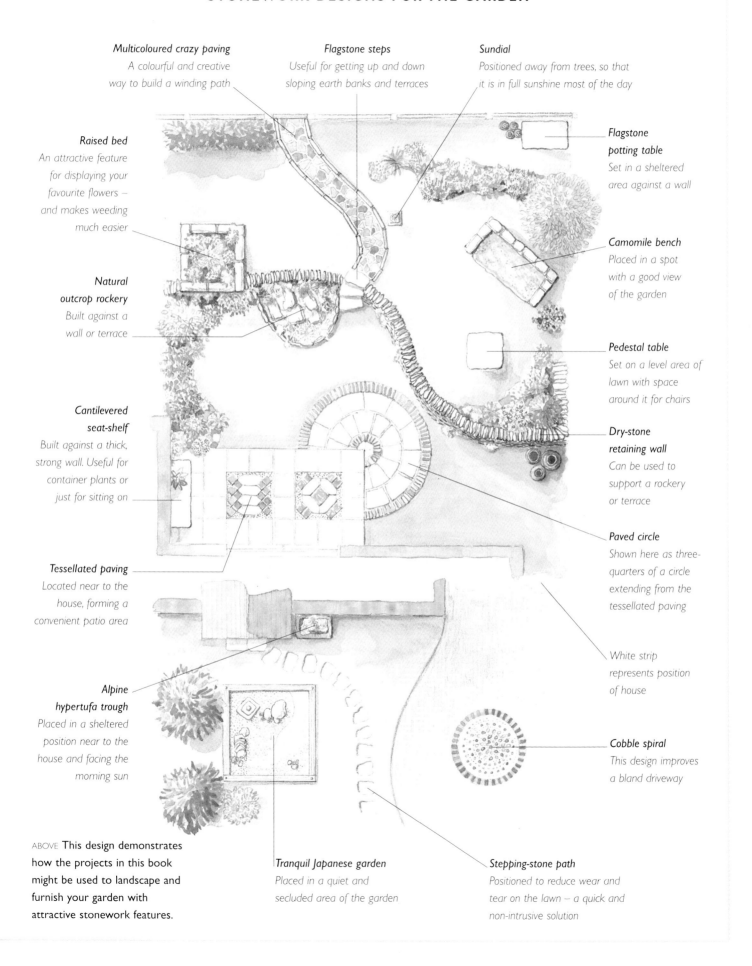

Multicoloured crazy paving
A colourful and creative way to build a winding path

Flagstone steps
Useful for getting up and down sloping earth banks and terraces

Sundial
Positioned away from trees, so that it is in full sunshine most of the day

Raised bed
An attractive feature for displaying your favourite flowers – and makes weeding much easier

Flagstone potting table
Set in a sheltered area against a wall

Camomile bench
Placed in a spot with a good view of the garden

Natural outcrop rockery
Built against a wall or terrace

Pedestal table
Set on a level area of lawn with space around it for chairs

Cantilevered seat-shelf
Built against a thick, strong wall. Useful for container plants or just for sitting on

Dry-stone retaining wall
Can be used to support a rockery or terrace

Paved circle
Shown here as three-quarters of a circle extending from the tessellated paving

Tessellated paving
Located near to the house, forming a convenient patio area

White strip represents position of house

Alpine hypertufa trough
Placed in a sheltered position near to the house and facing the morning sun

Cobble spiral
This design improves a bland driveway

Tranquil Japanese garden
Placed in a quiet and secluded area of the garden

Stepping-stone path
Positioned to reduce wear and tear on the lawn – a quick and non-intrusive solution

ABOVE **This design demonstrates how the projects in this book might be used to landscape and furnish your garden with attractive stonework features.**

Tools

The secret of tackling the projects successfully is using the correct tools for the job. A top-quality tool will make a huge difference to the ease with which a task can be accomplished. It is altogether more comfortable to hold, longer lasting, and ensures that tasks are completed in as short a time as possible.

TOOLS FOR HANDLING STONE

Gloves

Bucket

Sack barrow

Wheelbarrow

Protecting your feet and hands

Wear solid leather workboots, preferably with reinforced steel toecaps, to prevent your feet from getting squashed by a stray dropped stone, and work-gloves to save your hands from getting cut, abraded and otherwise damaged. The gloves might take a while to get used to, but they will protect your hands from the relentless wear and tear that is involved in working with a hammer and chisel, lifting stones and mixing sand and cement.

Making the work easier

Of all the tools you can buy, it is the wheelbarrow, sack barrow and bucket that make life easier when tackling stonework. By the time you get to the end of a project you will have formed a deep and loving relationship with both your wheelbarrow and sack barrow! A good wheelbarrow will save your back from a huge amount of stress and strain. If you buy one with a large inflated rubber tyre, and a tip-stop bar that protrudes in front, you will be able to bounce your way up steps and over rocks, and just as

easily be able to stop and tip out the load from the barrow. The wheelbarrow is used primarily for transporting wet and dry granular materials such as loose earth, sand, gravel and concrete.

A sack barrow is used for moving single, heavy items such as bags of cement, flagstones or large chunks of stone. It works on the lever principle, enabling you to lift and move weights that would otherwise be completely unmanageable. To use it, you nudge the platform under the item to be moved, pull back on the handles so that the weight is sitting over the wheels (over the fulcrum), then go on your way. A good, strong sack barrow will, depending upon the mass of the object, allow you to move anything up to 150–200 kg in weight with ease.

Finally, you need three or four plastic buckets. Don't bother about buying good-quality items, because buckets are more or less disposable – just buy the cheapest that you can find and use them until they fall apart. Some suppliers will cut the price if you purchase in multiples. Buckets are used for a variety of tasks, including transporting water for mixing into mortar and concrete.

TOOLS FOR MEASURING AND MARKING

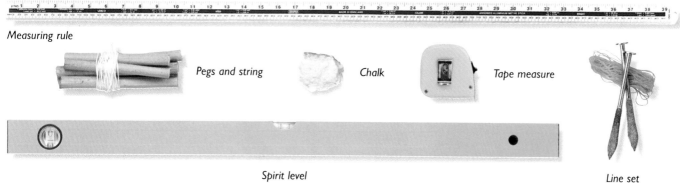

Measuring rule

Pegs and string

Chalk

Tape measure

Line set

Spirit level

Measuring

Ideally, you need two measuring tools – a flexible tape measure for setting out the site plan, and a rule for measuring individual rocks and blocks within the project. Make sure that both tools are marked out in metric and imperial, so that you can deal with products that are described in either system. If possible, buy a waterproof, fibreglass tape measure, as this will stand up better to the damp and dirt involved in stoneworking.

Marking out

The main tools are pegs and string for setting out the foundation on the ground, chalk for drawing a plan on a concrete base, and a spirit level for checking the horizontal and vertical levels within the structure. Buy one with a strong aluminium body. You may also wish to use a line set for guiding the courses of stone and esti-mating the course heights. The pegs are stuck into the ground (or a course), and the line stretched between them.

TOOLS FOR PREPARING A SITE

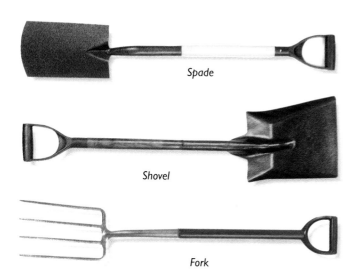

Spade

Shovel

Fork

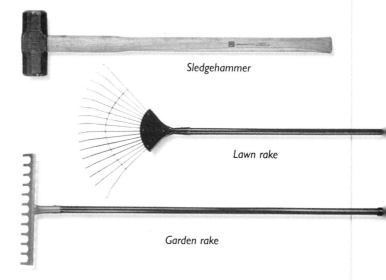

Sledgehammer

Lawn rake

Garden rake

Removing turf and digging earth

A spade is used to prepare the site. Having marked out the size of the foundation, take the spade, cut down through the thickness of the turf, and slice it into easy-to-manage squares. Scoop it straight into the wheelbarrow and remove it from the site. Finally, dig out the earth to the required depth and clean out to a flat base.

Compacting hardcore and raking

A sledgehammer will make short work of compacting hardcore. The smaller the stones, the easier it is to compact – builder's rubble requires a lot of effort, while crushed stone more or less puts itself into place. The procedure is simple: spread a thin layer

over the foundation area and pound it into place, walking back-wards and forwards over it from time to time.

The tool used for raking depends upon the material in ques-tion. It is best to use a fork for moving and breaking up clumps of earth, a garden rake for spreading gravel and shingle, and a lawn rake for spreading sand and for tidying up.

Mixing cement and moving gravel

The simplest way of mixing cement and moving gravel is to use a carefully chosen, good-quality shovel. Wash the shovel after mixing cement. Never try shovelling with a spade, or digging with a shovel – both exercises are a back-breaking waste of time!

TOOLS FOR SHAPING STONE

Mason's hammer

Angle grinder

Cold chisel

Bolster chisel

Club hammer

Breaking stone

One of the most direct ways of shaping or truing up stone (meaning to tap off a corner or shape an edge) is to use a mason's hammer, sometimes known as a brick hammer. The hammer is used on its own, without a chisel of any description. Cradle the stone (in your hand, on soft ground, or on a pad) and strike it repeatedly, working in a line. Flip it over and repeat the procedure on the other side, until the waste piece falls away.

To trim an edge back to a drawn line, the mason's hammer can again be used alone. Hold the stone with the edge to be worked nearest to you, and then hit it with a series of rapid pecks, so that the waste falls away as chips. If you find that you enjoy working with stone, and decide that you are going to try lots of the projects, it would be a good idea to get yourself a stout leather bib apron, as added protection from flying slivers of stone.

Cutting stone

While breaking stone with a mason's hammer is relatively approximate, cutting stone is a more accurate procedure that involves using a club hammer with a bolster chisel or a cold chisel.

The bolster chisel is used for hefty tasks such as chopping a stone in half. To cut a stone down the run of the grain – in much the same way as splitting a log – you simply set the chisel on the end grain and work backwards and forwards until you see the stone begin to fracture. You

then work away at a crack until the stone splits into two pieces. To break a large stone across the run of the grain – like cutting a long log into two lengths – draw a line with chalk, and hit it with the club hammer and bolster chisel. Repeatedly work around all the faces until the stone falls into two.

A cold chisel is appropriate for more delicate tasks, such as trimming an edge, or other fine adjustments.

Sawing stone

In the context of this book, sawing stone involves using an electric angle grinder to cut flagstone slabs. The grinder is first fitted with a stone-cutting disc, as described by the manufacturer. You must wear a dust-mask, a pair of goggles, gloves and stout workboots. The grinder is connected up to a 110 volt power supply by means of a yellow-box transformer. The disc is placed on the drawn line and the tool is run forward to make the cut. As the angle grinder creates an enormous amount of dust, it is best to work outside, setting the stone down flat on the grass and holding it with your foot (keeping it well away from the line of cut). It does not matter if the disc slips off at the end of the line, because it simply cuts into the grass and no damage is done. If you feel at all unhappy about the prospect of using an angle grinder, ask a knowledgeable friend to show you how to do it. Never use a grinder if you are tired or in any way under stress.

CAUTION

It is vital to wear goggles for all stone-breaking and cutting operations, to protect your eyes from dust, chips of stone and fragments of metal. Wear a dust-mask when using the angle grinder.

TOOLS FOR CONCRETE AND MORTAR

Mortar float

Bricklayer's trowel

Pointing trowel

Spreading concrete and mortar

If you want to achieve a smooth finish once the concrete or mortar has been tipped into place, you have to use a mortar float or plasterer's trowel. Made from steel, wood or plastic, the float is used with an even, side to side smoothing action – in much the same way as you use a bricklayer's trowel. If you want the water to rise to the surface (to create an ultra-smooth finish), use a steel float, otherwise one made from plastic or wood will suffice. Always clean the float under running water after use, especially on the underside and around the handle.

Handling mortar

The bricklayer's trowel is designed for transferring large slaps of mortar. The pointing trowel is shaped for pointing, and for raking out some of the mortar from between the courses for decorative effect. Many beginners find it easier to use the smaller pointing trowel for both tasks. Use the tool that you feel comfortable with and change over if and when you feel the need. Many people find that although the large trowel certainly gets the mortar shifted quickly, its weight puts a strain on the wrist. Make sure that your chosen trowel has a well-shaped handle, which feels good to hold.

TOOLS FOR FINISHING A PROJECT

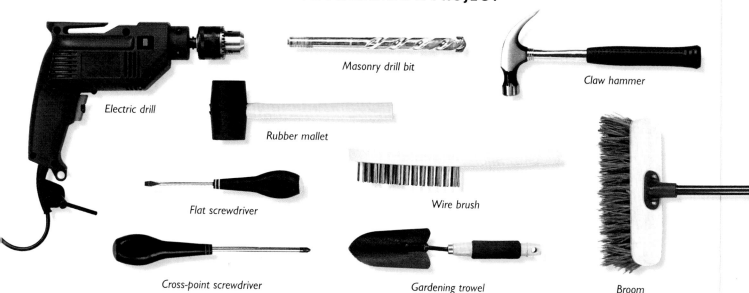

Masonry drill bit

Claw hammer

Electric drill

Rubber mallet

Flat screwdriver

Wire brush

Cross-point screwdriver

Gardening trowel

Broom

Holes and fixings

Stonework also involves drilling holes, banging in nails, and driving in screws. It is best to use an electric drill in conjunction with a masonry drill bit for boring holes into rock, a carpenter's claw hammer for nailing foundation frames, and both flat and cross-point screwdrivers for pushing home the screws. If a giant-size electric drill is required, rent it by the day from a hire shop.

Levelling and cleaning

You may find a rubber mallet useful for nudging individual stones into place. A wire brush is excellent for cleaning stray blobs of mortar from the stone when the mortaring process is finished. At the end of a long day's work, a good, stiff-bristled bass broom makes it much easier to get through the tedious task of tidying up. Wash the broom after use to remove grit and grime from the head and handle, and store it with the head uppermost, so the bristles have a chance to dry out.

Planting

A gardening trowel is needed for planting a selection of plants in projects such as the Natural Outcrop Rockery (page 42) and the Raised Bed (page 52). It is also a handy little tool for scooping up small amounts of sand and cement. Buy a couple of them and use them for the various tasks.

Materials

We are not concerned about the geological make-up of the various materials – apart from identification, it does not contribute anything to the projects to know whether a rock is igneous or metamorphic. We have concentrated on the common names and the working characteristics of the rocks.

NATURAL STONE

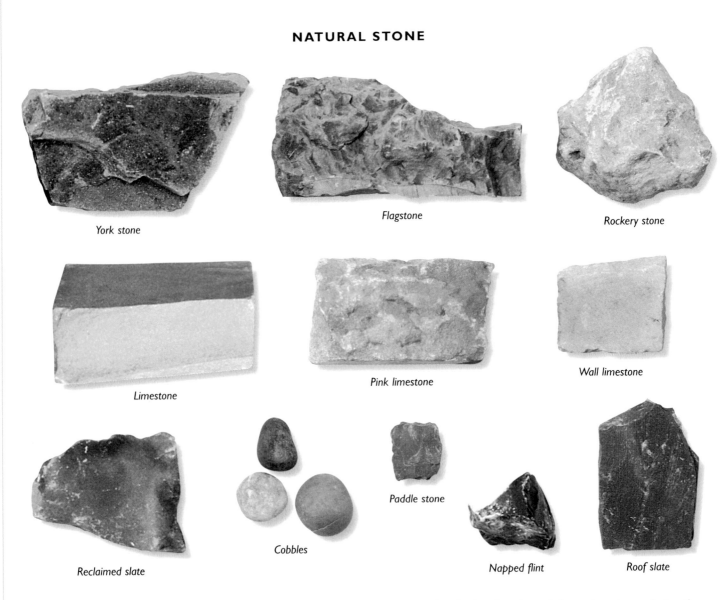

York stone

Flagstone

Rockery stone

Limestone

Pink limestone

Wall limestone

Reclaimed slate

Cobbles

Paddle stone

Napped flint

Roof slate

Limestone

Limestone was once very popular as a building stone, because it is easy to shape, in any direction, to make steps, slabs and blocks. However, there are now so many reconstituted stone look-alike "limestone" blocks on the market, that the genuine item has fallen from favour. While it is prohibitively expensive to use new sawn and faced limestone, salvaged architectural limestone is reasonably priced. When we needed cut blocks of white stone to make the Japanese lantern for the Tranquil Japanese Garden (page 82), we found salvaged limestone to be by far the best option, because it had the most attractive appearance.

Always identify the direction of the grain prior to laying the blocks, making sure that the layers within the grain sit horizontally rather than vertically. If you are not sure which way the grain runs, look very closely at the salvaged stone to see how the various faces were arranged in their previous setting, and then simply copy the arrangement in your project.

Sandstone

Sandstone and limestone are both formed by deposition – meaning that the stone is created from layers of material put under enormous pressure. Limestone is made up of organic remains such as shell and bones, and sandstone is particles of quartz or sand. Sandstone ranges in colour from pinky-red and brown through to black, green and blue-grey. Some stones are so hard that they ring when struck, while others are so soft and crumbly that they can be broken like dry biscuits. Depending upon the variety, sandstone is good for dry-stone walling, stepping stones and flagstones. Always avoid stone that flakes when touched, as it is likely to have been damaged by frost.

Slate

The geological formation of slate is the result of the heating of clay deposits under pressure. Slate is characterized by its blue, black or green colour, and smooth, shiny surface. It can be split into thin sheets, which are mainly used for roofing.

In this book, slate is used in the form of small pucks of "paddle" stone sold by quarries, and as broken roof stone sold by architectural salvage companies. While slate does not easily blend in with limestone and sandstone, so it cannot be used in large lumps in equal partnership, small pieces make an effective colour contrast. For example, the Flagstone Potting Table (page 108) uses thin layers of slate with deeply raked joints to contrast with the rather severe blocks of limestone. Be aware, when you are choosing your stone, that the terms "slate" and "roofing stone" are commonly interchanged and used to describe all manner of stone types that can be broken into thin sheets.

Granite

While there is no denying that granite is immensely strong and attractive in both colour and texture – ranging from dark green-blue through to a pinkish grey – it is also so hard that it is almost impossible to work. Certainly you can just about make headway with a grinder, and sometimes you can be lucky with a hammer and bolster chisel, but mostly it is too difficult to cut. If you really want to use granite, search out pieces in the stoneyard that suit your needs as they stand. For example, you could use salvaged road blocks and kerbstones to build the lantern in the Tranquil Japanese Garden (page 82), or setts to edge the Paved Circle (page 70), massive pieces of quarry stone as feature stones in the Natural Outcrop Rockery (page 42), or even large salvaged field posts as guardians or sentinels. Be very wary about obtaining pieces of granite that are bigger than you need, because they are usually so impossible to work that the task is not worth the wear and tear on your tools. One of the best ways of using granite is in its crushed state, as a decorative spread.

RECONSTITUTED STONE

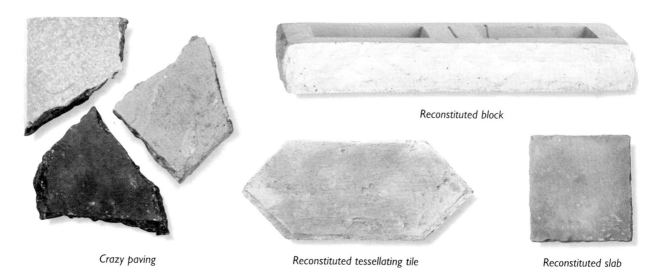

Reconstituted block

Crazy paving

Reconstituted tessellating tile

Reconstituted slab

Reconstituted blocks

Reconstituted stone blocks are concrete blocks – sometimes made with an aggregate containing the stone that they seek to imitate – that are made to look like natural stone. There are double-sided blocks that imitate rough-tooled limestone, blocks that look like fieldstone, blocks that resemble sawn limestone, and so on. In many instances, you can cut costs by collecting the blocks direct from the manufacturer.

You may wish to substitute reconstituted blocks in the projects to save money, but they are usually not as beautiful as the real thing. The best way to regard them is as a little taster that will lead you into the more exciting adventure of using natural stone.

Reconstituted slabs

While reconstituted blocks can look quite crude, reconstituted slabs, on the other hand, are a great idea. Made in much the same way as the blocks, often with an aggregate containing the stone that they are masquerading as, many reconstituted slabs are so convincing that at first sight they cannot be distinguished from the real thing. Such slabs come in all sorts of shapes, sizes, colours and textures: tessellating shapes that look like red quarry tiles, sandstone paving slabs, on-edge stone and brick slabs, limestone and sandstone flagstones, and many other forms and designs. If you want to cut costs, they can be substituted when a project calls for thin layers of stone. Pick slabs that are described as "colour-fast".

CHIPS, GRAVEL, GRIT, CEMENT AND LIME

Limestone chips

Smooth gravel

Pink gravel

Medium gravel

Pea gravel

Oyster shell

Sharp sand

Sand and gravel

Soft sand

Cement

Lime

CAUTION

Cement and lime are corrosive and can seriously burn the skin. Always wear goggles and gloves, and wash your hands and face after working with them.

Soft sand

Soft sand, sometimes called builder's sand, is used for making smooth-textured mortar. Sold by the bag or lorry-load, the colour and texture of the soft sand on offer will usually relate to the colour of the stone in your area. If you are building with local stone, it is best to use local soft sand. However, builder's suppliers purchase some sand from far-distant quarries, so you do have to check the colour of your intended purchase to make sure it is suitable. If you are looking for good colour and low cost, your best option is to order your sand in bulk from a local pit.

Always make sure that the sand has been well washed and is free from salt and particles of clay. Salt damages mortar and concrete. If the sand smells rank, or contains animal or vegetable matter, or looks in any way contaminated, go to another supplier.

Sharp sand

Sharp sand is nearly always used for making concrete, and is also added to soft sand to make a coarse, bulky mortar. In terms of colour and cost, much the same can be said for sharp sand as for soft. Whether the sand comes from a pit, quarry or river, or is a mixture of naturally occurring sand and crushed stone, it is vital that it is free from clay, loam and organic matter.

Check it if you have any doubts: clean sand will not stain your fingers, and if you put it in a glass of water, shake it up and leave it to stand, you should end up with just a thin film of silt on top of the sand, and clear water. If there is a layer of scum floating on the water and a salty smell – a bit like a beach at low tide – then the chances are that it is unwashed sea sand, which is totally unsuitable for making mortar and concrete.

Cement

Cement powder – sold in 25 kg and 50 kg bags, and described generically as "Portland cement" – is one of the chief ingredients of mortar and concrete. Though it is undoubtedly true to say that you can save money by ordering a large number of 50 kg bags, this is the one instance where it is much better to buy just enough for the job in hand. Not only are 50 kg bags difficult to handle, but they are also flimsy and liable to tear, the cement powder is susceptible to damp, and loose powder is highly corrosive and very bad for the skin, eyes and lungs.

Lime

Lime is used together with cement and sand to make mortar. Though a "cement mortar" can be made without lime (undoubtedly harder and stronger than lime and cement mortar), it is also so hard that it stains the stone and pulls it apart. As with cement powder, it is best to order lime in small quantities and to store it in a dry place. Lime is highly corrosive, to the extent that you should wear goggles and a mask when mixing, and gloves for general handling. If you are mixing on a windy day, when the lime is blowing about, wash your face and hands afterwards.

Aggregates

Concrete consists of Portland cement, and a mixture of sand and stone known as an aggregate. The shape and size of the particles of sand and stone within the aggregate decide the character of the concrete – meaning its strength, hardness, durability and porosity.

Commonly, aggregate is made up from graded 2–3 mm sand, broken stone and various types of crushed and graded gravel. For the projects in this book, choose an average mix made up from small-sized gravel and sand. If you want to make a very coarse concrete, for a thin levelling slab, you can bulk out your mix by adding a small amount of crushed brick or broken stone – just break it up with a hammer, damp it down, and add it to the mix.

Gravel, limestone chips or oyster shell may also be laid down as a decorative surface. Choose a fine gravel such as pea gravel for a delicate appearance; limestone chips provide a chunkier effect. Gravel colour depends on the stone it is made from.

OTHER MATERIALS

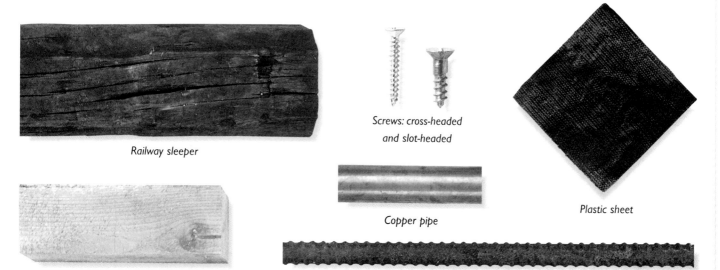

Railway sleeper

Screws: cross-headed and slot-headed

Plastic sheet

Rough-sawn pine section

Copper pipe

Iron reinforcing bar

Wood and fixings

Foundation frames should be made up from rough-sawn softwood, as sold by most garden centres. Do not worry too much about the quality of the wood or the length of time it has been seasoned – other than to see that it is reasonably strong along its length. To fix these temporary frames, you can use a mixture of screws and nails, or whatever comes to hand. It's a good idea to use high-quality, pressure-treated wood to make the frame for the Tranquil Japanese Garden (page 82).

The lengths of railway sleeper used under the Alpine Hypertufa Trough (page 62), and for bending the copper pipe in the Cantilevered Seat-Shelf (page 96), can be obtained as small offcuts. Avoid railway sleepers that ooze tar or creosote – they will ruin the tools and stain your hands and clothes.

Metal and plastics

The iron bar and copper pipe used for the Cantilevered Seat-Shelf (page 96) can be obtained from a builder's merchant as inexpensive offcuts. The iron bar is sold as reinforcement bar or "rebar", while the copper tube is used for plumbing. The plastic sheet used under the Tranquil Japanese Garden (page 82) is available from builder's merchants, plastics suppliers or garden centres.

If you are keen to cut down on costs, visit the nearest building site and see if the site manager can spare you any scraps. If you are successful in your quest, before you take your haul away it's a good idea to ask the site manager to sign a note to the effect that the materials have been given to you, just in case you are questioned by the site security guards. Scrap metal merchants may also be willing to let you have small items free of charge.

Mixing mortar and concrete

Stonework involves the frequent mixing of mortar (for laying stone) and concrete (for foundations). If you can achieve a mix with a good texture, colour and working consistency, the construction process will go smoothly. Follow the old adage that says, "Mixing a little not a lot, gets the job done in half the time".

MIXING A SMALL AMOUNT OF MORTAR IN A WHEELBARROW

Mixing procedure

1 Use a shovel to carefully measure the dry ingredients into the wheelbarrow – first the sand, then the Portland cement and the lime. Continue until the barrow is about half-full. Turn the ingredients over several times until they are thoroughly mixed.

2 Pour about one-third of a bucket of water into one end of the wheelbarrow, then drag small amounts of the dry mix into the water. Repeat the process until all the water has been soaked up by the dry mix.

3 Turn over the whole heap several times, all the while adding small amounts of water, until you can chop it into clean, wet slices.

Mixing
Drag the dry mix
into the water

ABOVE It is often convenient to use a wheelbarrow for mixing mortar – bear in mind that you will need to give it a good clean afterwards.

MIXING A COARSE LIME AND CEMENT MORTAR

This mortar is made up of a 50/50 mixture of soft sand and sharp sand, Portland cement and lime. Because it is coarse, it is good for filling large gaps and wide courses. Measure the dry ingredients on to a board with a shovel – first the sand, then the cement and lime. Mix it up, dig a hole in the centre, and pour in about half a bucket of water. Work round the heap, dragging small amounts of the dry mix into the water. If the water threatens to break over the rim, swiftly pull in more of the dry mix to stem the flow. When the water has been soaked up, add more until the mortar is the correct consistency. The finished mixture should form crisp, firm slices that stand up under their own weight without crumbling.

MIXING CONCRETE FOR FOUNDATION FOOTINGS

A concrete suitable for foundations contains cement, sharp sand and aggregate. With a shovel, measure the sand and the Portland cement on to the board. Turn over the mixture thoroughly, until it is well blended. Dig a hole in the centre of the mound, pour in about half a bucket of water, and then gradually drag the dry mix into the water. Continue until you achieve a wet, sloppy mixture. Finally, measure in the aggregate. Carry on turning it over and adding small amounts of water until a shovelful of the mixture holds its shape when it is formed into a ridge.

MORTAR AND CONCRETE MIXES

Smooth lime and cement mortar

Lime and cement mortar, suitable for fine- to medium-course stonework, is made up from 2 parts Portland cement, 1 part lime and 9 parts soft sand. The sand should be chosen to complement the colour of the stone.

Coarse lime and cement mortar

A coarse lime and cement mortar, appropriate for bulking out wide courses, can be constructed from 2 parts cement, 1 part lime, 4 parts soft sand and 4 parts sharp sand. The proportion of sharp sand to soft sand should be modified to suit the texture of your chosen stone.

Concrete for foundations

A good, general-purpose concrete, suitable for small footings and foundations, is made of 1 part Portland cement, 2 parts sharp sand and 3 parts aggregate. (The aggregate is made up from gravel graded to pass through a 25 mm sieve.)

Moving stone

Even though we live in an age of cranes and hoists, you will almost certainly have to physically move the stone by hand from the driveway, where it has been delivered, to the site in the garden. This section shows you how to do it with ease. But if you suspect that a stone is too heavy, ask a friend to help rather than risking injury.

MOVING HEAVY SLABS

Moving the slab
Rock the slab on to one corner and pivot it round

Use rough board to protect lawns

Moving procedure

1 Slabs weigh about 150–200 kg, so ask a friend to help you. First, use a sledgehammer to bang a couple of wooden wedges under one edge of the slab to lift it about 70 mm off the ground. Put two wooden boards on the ground in the spot where the slab will be. Leave a small gap between them.

2 Together, grip the jacked-up edge of the stone (the stronger person being ready to push, and the other person ready to pull and steady). Heave the stone upright until it is standing on edge.

3 Rock the slab on to one of the bottom corners and pivot it so that the raised corner is pointing in the direction of the site. Lower this corner, then swing the other corner around, "walking" the slab across the garden. Keep stopping to rest along the way.

4 When you have reached the new location, lower the stone on to the wooden boards (these maintain a gap between the stone and the ground, preventing your hands from getting trapped). Lift an edge and ease the boards out.

MOVING HEAVY ROCKERY STONES

Moving procedure

1 Having asked a friend to help, take a solid metal wheelbarrow (one with a large pneumatic tyre) and wheel it up to the stone. Lie it on its side with one edge alongside the stone.

2 Place a pad of old carpet between the stone and the wheelbarrow, then manoeuvre the stone into the wheelbarrow. One of you eases the stone and the other holds the wheelbarrow.

3 When the stone is in the wheelbarrow, push and pull the wheelbarrow into an upright position, working together. Ease the stone to lie over the wheel. Always be ready to steady the wheelbarrow during its journey.

RIGHT Roll heavy stones if possible, rather than lifting them. To protect your back when you have to lift a heavy weight, keep your knees bent, with your spine upright, and your weight balanced over your feet.

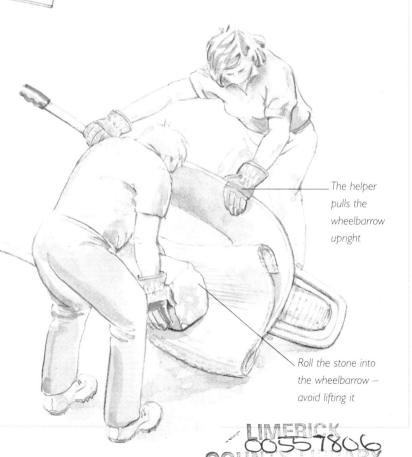

The helper pulls the wheelbarrow upright

Roll the stone into the wheelbarrow – avoid lifting it

Cutting stone

In many ways, the art and craft of good stonework is concerned with fitting and using stone as you find it but, when there is no other option other than to make a cut, the main part of the challenge is getting it right. Today, much cutting is done with an electric angle grinder but traditional chisels are still required for some tasks.

CUTTING STONE USING AN ANGLE GRINDER

Choosing the correct angle grinder

Angle grinders are deceptively easy to use, but it is important to choose the correct grinder for your needs. While it is generally much easier to use a heavy-duty 230 mm-diameter grinder than it is to use a lightweight 115 mm-diameter model, most beginners are not going to get much use out of a large grinder. It is best to hire various grinders to start with, and see how you get on.

Pay great attention to the serious business of safety. You need goggles to guard your eyes against fragments of stone, metal and dust, a dust-mask to protect your lungs from stone dust, ear defenders to shield your ears from noise, gloves to ward off splinters, and stout boots to armour your feet.

When you are ready to make a cut, switch on the power and move the machine forwards, all the time remaining ready to resist kickback.

Choosing and fitting the cutting disc

Select a stone-cutting disc to fit your grinder. Disconnect the power cable, turn the spindle over by hand, and press in the lock button until the spindle stays put. Unscrew the clamping ring, slide on the correct disc, replace the ring and use the special wrench to tighten up. Release the lock button and turn over the disc by hand to ensure it does not wobble or scrape. When you are happy that everything is correctly and safely assembled, you are ready to turn on the power and make the cut.

The correct working set-up

When using an angle grinder, it is a good idea to ask a helper to be present in case of any problems. First, establish a working area on the lawn, and ban children and pets.

Set the slab to be worked on the ground. Make sure that none of your helpers is standing in front of the line of cut. Keep your feet well away from the cutting line. On no account kneel in line with the cutter, in case it slips. Never try to force the pace of the machine, and never twist the disc. If the cutting wheel looks in any way chipped, cracked, or warped, change to a new disc.

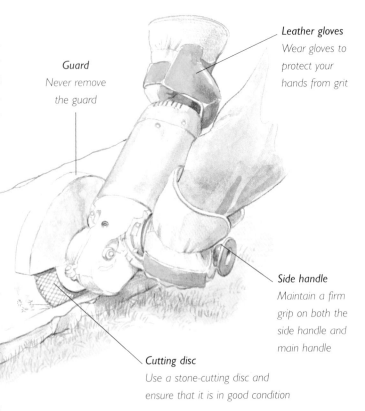

Guard
Never remove the guard

Leather gloves
Wear gloves to protect your hands from grit

Side handle
Maintain a firm grip on both the side handle and main handle

Cutting disc
Use a stone-cutting disc and ensure that it is in good condition

ABOVE Take the utmost care when using an angle grinder: it is a potentially dangerous tool. Follow safety procedures carefully.

Cutting procedure

1 Set the slab down flat on the grass and draw out the line of cut with a tape measure, chalk and straight-edge. Check that the grinder is in good working order, and kit yourself out with goggles, a dust-mask, thick leather gloves and stout boots. It is advisable to wear ear defenders too.

2 Hold the grinder so that the wheel is at right angles to the slab. Brace yourself, and, keeping your feet well out of the way, switch on the power. Hold the spinning disc to the chalk line and carefully make a light, scoring cut.

3 Make several runs to deepen the line of cut, then switch off the power and flip the slab over on the grass. Switch the power back on and re-run the whole procedure on the other side. Continue repeating the process until the slab breaks into two.

CUTTING STONE USING CHISELS

Using the bolster chisel

Bolster chisels are used for breaking and cutting stone. Purchase the best chisel that you can find – ideally one that has been drop-forged, hardened and tempered, and fitted with a one-piece moulded plastic protective grip. Take the club hammer and a piece of stone, and experiment with various cuts and blows. The first thing you will observe is that the angle of the chisel, in relation to the weight of the blow, is critical to the cut. For example, a light, tentative tap with the chisel held at right angles to the stone will result in a chip, while a heavy, decisive blow will result in a fracture. If you want to trim an edge, you angle the chisel towards the edge, lower it slightly, and then make the blow. The edge will break away, leaving a peak on the edge face. By adjusting the angle of the chisel, it is possible to change the shape of the edge peak.

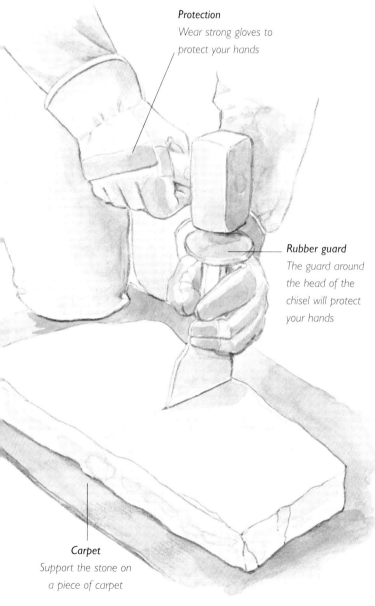

Protection
Wear strong gloves to
protect your hands

Rubber guard
The guard around
the head of the
chisel will protect
your hands

Carpet
Support the stone on
a piece of carpet

ABOVE **Cutting stone using a bolster chisel and club hammer.**
Hold the chisel firmly on the mark and deliver a well-aimed blow.

Using the cold chisel

Cold chisels are used for more delicate cutting tasks than bolster chisels. Purchase a top-quality 25 mm-wide chisel – choose one that has been drop-forged, hardened and tempered. Support a slab of stone on a pad and use the club hammer to try out various cuts. To trim an edge, hold the chisel at a very low angle to the stone, with the cutting edge looking to the edge of the stone, then make a light blow so that the waste breaks away as a chip rather than a chunk. Experiment with various angles and the weight of strike, until you can, to some extent, predict the outcome.

Sharpening chisels

Drag and roll the end of the chisel against the grindstone until the ragged edge has been ground to a mitred bevel. Grind the cutting edge back to the original angle of about 60 degrees, continually dipping the tool into water to prevent the steel from overheating.

Cutting a stone in two

1 Chalk the line of cut on both sides of the stone, and put the stone on something soft to help absorb the shock – such as a pad of old carpet, a pile of sand, or the lawn. Make sure that you are wearing goggles and strong leather gloves.
2 Take a bolster chisel in one hand and a club hammer in the other, and make a series of light passes to score the line. Do this three times, all the while increasing the power of the blows.
3 Repeat the procedure on the other side of the stone, and then after about three passes, strike the chisel with maximum force until the stone breaks along the line.

HOW TO AVOID TOO MUCH CUTTING

Fitting is better than cutting
The secret of good stonework is, as far as possible, to use the stone as you find it. Choose your stone with great care, spending a long time selecting pieces for the best possible fit. If you work in this way, all you will have to do is to slightly modify edges and corners so that the pieces fit snugly alongside one another. Always try to fit rather than cut.

Striking blows
When you have decided on the position of the cutting line, set the edge of the chisel on the mark and strike it with a club hammer. Repeat this procedure until the cut has been made. A single, well-aimed blow with the hammer is many times more effective than lots of little misaligned taps.

Working with the grain
Study the stone carefully and identify the grain, or strata lines. Try, as far as possible, to align your cuts with the run of the grain. This ensures the stone cuts cleanly.

Making foundations

Every stone structure starts with a foundation ranging from gravel through to crushed stone, compacted

hardcore and concrete. This section shows you how to select the option that suits your needs. It is important not

to skimp on quantities. If in doubt, make a foundation bigger rather than smaller.

TYPES OF GROUND AND FOUNDATION REQUIREMENTS

Inspecting the site

Have a good look at the site. Dig a small hole to see what it is like under the topsoil. Is it hard and rocky, or is it soft and squashy? Is there a lot of rock and rubble on site? Is it well drained or boggy? In the light of your survey, and in the knowledge that the options for a foundation range from a trench filled with gravel, through to a trench with compacted hardcore and layer of stone, or a trench with compacted hardcore and a layer of concrete, or various combinations of these, spend time considering your needs.

For example, if you wanted to build the Camomile Bench on page 114, and you have a dry, rocky site, you could get away with an 80 mm slab of concrete and a shallow layer of concrete. But on a wet site, you would need to dig a trench about 300 mm deep, half-fill it with gravel for drainage, and then top it off with a generous layer of concrete.

If you are unsure what sort of drainage your site has, dig a trial hole, fill it with water, and see how long it takes to drain away.

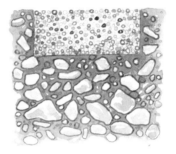

LEFT **A gravel footpath needs no foundation if it is set in a well-drained, compacted soil. The gravel is adequately contained.**

LEFT **A compacted hardcore foundation for a concrete footpath. This is suitable for soil with moderate drainage.**

CONSTRUCTING A CONCRETE SLAB FOUNDATION

Building procedure

1 Carefully measure the site, bang in wooden pegs to mark the limits of the foundation, and run a string around the pegs. Remove the turf and dig down to a depth of about 250 mm. Clean the trench out to a level base. Move all the turf and the loose soil from the site.

2 Bang two wooden pegs into the trench base, positioned away from the sides as shown, so that they stand proud by about 200 mm (they are about 50 mm below the turf level). Bridge the pegs with a spirit level and make adjustments until they are at the same level. Try not to destroy the top of the pegs when hammering.

3 Half-fill the trench with hardcore and, being careful not to knock the pegs, compact it with a sledgehammer. Finally, top up the trench with concrete and tamp it level with a wooden beam. You should just be able to see the top of the pegs.

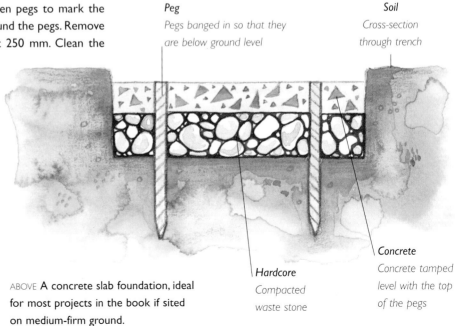

Peg
Pegs banged in so that they are below ground level

Soil
Cross-section through trench

Hardcore
Compacted waste stone

Concrete
Concrete tamped level with the top of the pegs

ABOVE **A concrete slab foundation, ideal for most projects in the book if sited on medium-firm ground.**

A ROCK AND RUBBLE FOUNDATION

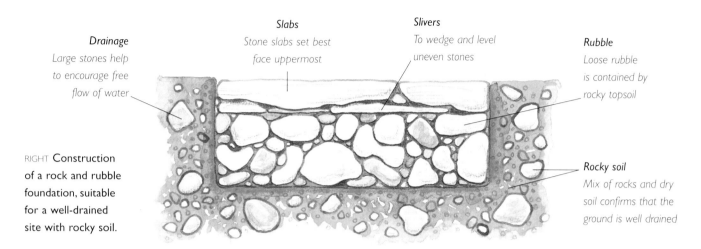

Drainage
Large stones help
to encourage free
flow of water

Slabs
Stone slabs set best
face uppermost

Slivers
To wedge and level
uneven stones

Rubble
Loose rubble
is contained by
rocky topsoil

RIGHT **Construction
of a rock and rubble
foundation, suitable
for a well-drained
site with rocky soil.**

Rocky soil
Mix of rocks and dry
soil confirms that the
ground is well drained

If you have a well-drained, rocky site, with a thin layer of topsoil, and a lot of loose stone and builder's rubble available, and you intend to build a project such as the the Dry-Stone Retaining Wall (page 88), you can easily get away without laying a concrete slab. Dig a trench to a depth of about 300 mm, and then systematically fill it with rock and rubble, all the while pounding it with the sledgehammer. When you get to within about 100 mm of ground level, carefully select large slabs of stone to cover the hardcore. Use small slivers and wedges of stone to adjust the level of the slabs so that they are firm and stable.

OTHER FOUNDATION EXAMPLES

If you have a well-drained site, you can lay a minimal foundation and top it off with a concrete slab. Let's say that you want to build the Pedestal Table on page 120. Dig a hole to a depth of about 400 mm and knock in four side pegs. Nail wooden battens to bridge pairs of pegs, keeping them at the same level, and finishing up with the battens just below turf level. Half-fill the trench with hardcore and fill with concrete, up to the level of the battens. Drag a tamping beam across to skim the concrete level. Be careful not to knock either the pegs or the battens out of alignment.

If you have a boggy site, you need to keep the foundation drained by digging two trenches for the hardcore. These are bridged and topped with a concrete slab.

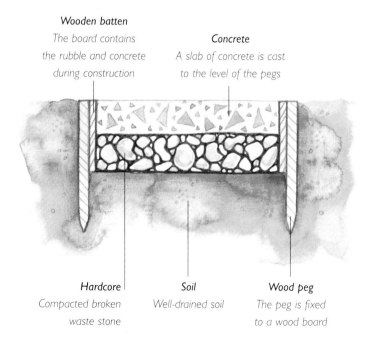

Wooden batten
The board contains
the rubble and concrete
during construction

Concrete
A slab of concrete is cast
to the level of the pegs

Hardcore
Compacted broken
waste stone

Soil
Well-drained soil

Wood peg
The peg is fixed
to a wood board

ABOVE **Use this foundation construction for well-drained sites. The surrounding soil needs to be reasonably compact and stable.**

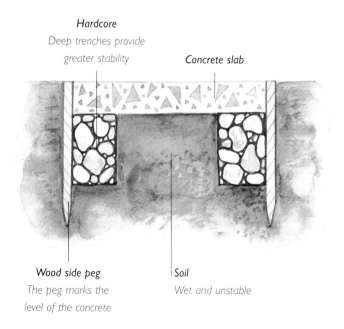

Hardcore
Deep trenches provide
greater stability

Concrete slab

Wood side peg
The peg marks the
level of the concrete

Soil
Wet and unstable

ABOVE **This type of construction is suited to soil that is boggy, loose and generally unstable. The hardcore walls provide good drainage.**

Paving and paths

Paving and paths not only enhance the garden in the sense that they are functionally desirable, they can also be visually exciting in terms of materials. Paths lead the eye – a path winding out of sight behind a hedge invites exploration and can impart an air of mystery. If you want to know more, keep reading.

DESIGNS FOR PATHS

ABOVE A gravel path edged with concrete "stone" blocks, which are supported by banked earth borders. The length of the kerb blocks defines the shape of the curve.

ABOVE Reconstituted stones or flagstones framed by rows of bricks set on their edge. There is plenty of design scope with various combinations of materials and patterns.

ABOVE Randomly-shaped stepping stones make an attractive feature, and are less intrusive than a solid path. The spaces between them must be equal.

Functional paths and paving

Have a look at your garden and consider how it might benefit from having one or more functional paths, or perhaps an area of utility paving. Perhaps you have trouble pushing your wheelbarrow down an existing path because it is too narrow? Would the vegetable garden be easier to work if it were divided up by a number of paths? Would it be a good idea to create a path along the shortest route from the back door to the compost heap? Do you want to avoid having to tiptoe across a muddy lawn? Do you wish that a particular area was dry so that children could play on it? Do you want a path wide enough for a wheelchair?

Designer paths and paving

The purpose of a designer path is not necessarily to take the shortest possible route, or even to provide a surface that is smooth and dry, but rather to provide the user with an exciting, dynamic, tactile and visual experience. Ideas such as irregular stepping stones that curve across the lawn and disappear behind a shrub, the feel and sound of gravel underfoot, an area of paving that is decorated with an inset design, a paved circle with a bench seat – all encourage visitors to change pace and appreciate their surroundings. Well thought-out designer paths and areas of paving can enhance the landscape, adding shape, colour, texture and mystery to the composition of the garden.

Think how a path or an area of paving might improve your enjoyment of the garden. A paved circle would allow you to sit outside on a warm summer's evening. Or you could build a crazy paving path to wander around the rockery and on to a camomile bench. Maybe you could design a combined path and paved circle, which could include a stone seat and barbecue. Your challenge may be a path that encircles the house, or a path that wanders off into the woods. The possibilities are endless.

FLAGSTONE PATH CONSTRUCTION

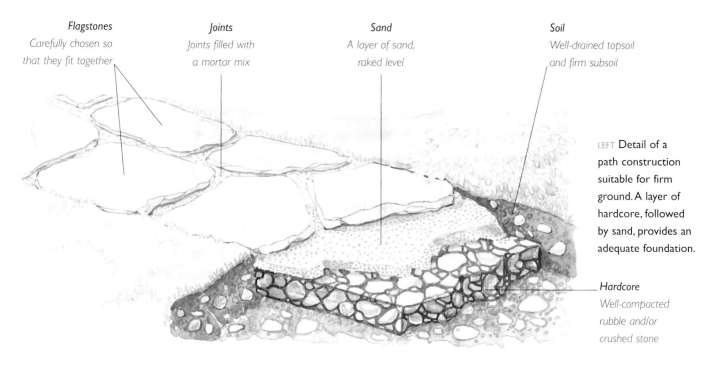

Flagstones
*Carefully chosen so
that they fit together*

Joints
*Joints filled with
a mortar mix*

Sand
*A layer of sand,
raked level*

Soil
*Well-drained topsoil
and firm subsoil*

LEFT Detail of a
path construction
suitable for firm
ground. A layer of
hardcore, followed
by sand, provides an
adequate foundation.

Hardcore
*Well-compacted
rubble and/or
crushed stone*

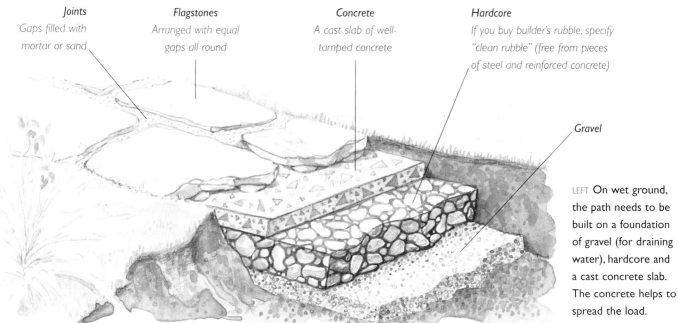

Joints
*Gaps filled with
mortar or sand*

Flagstones
*Arranged with equal
gaps all round*

Concrete
*A cast slab of well-
tamped concrete*

Hardcore
*If you buy builder's rubble, specify
"clean rubble" (free from pieces
of steel and reinforced concrete)*

Gravel

LEFT On wet ground,
the path needs to be
built on a foundation
of gravel (for draining
water), hardcore and
a cast concrete slab.
The concrete helps to
spread the load.

Flagstone paths on firm ground

If the ground is stony and well drained, and you plan to use good-size flagstones, it is only necessary to build a foundation of hardcore topped off with a layer of sand.

Dig a trench to a depth of about 200 mm and half-fill it with well-compacted builder's rubble or crushed stone, to a thickness of 100 mm. Top this with a 50 mm-thick bed of well-raked, level sand, and then set the stones in place. Brush sand, containing a mixture of grass and flower seeds, between the joints. This will encourage the ingress of plants to bind the stones firmly together.

Flagstone paths on wet ground

When the ground is soft and badly drained, and you want to use flagstones, you need to build a foundation of gravel covered by well-compacted hardcore and concrete.

Dig a trench to a depth of about 250 mm and fill it with gravel to a thickness of 50 mm. Spread builder's rubble or crushed stone over the gravel to a thickness of 100 mm. Finally, top the hardcore with a 50 mm-thick bed of well-tamped concrete, and set the stone in place. Brush sand between the joints. The gravel foundation base will allow water to drain under the path.

Rock gardens

The whole subject of building rock gardens and arranging stone is so subjective that it is difficult to offer advice.

Go and look at other gardens, touch as many stones as you can, take a trip to a rocky beach or a mountain slope

to get inspiration from the natural landscape, and then decide what appeals to you.

ROCKERY DESIGN AND SITING

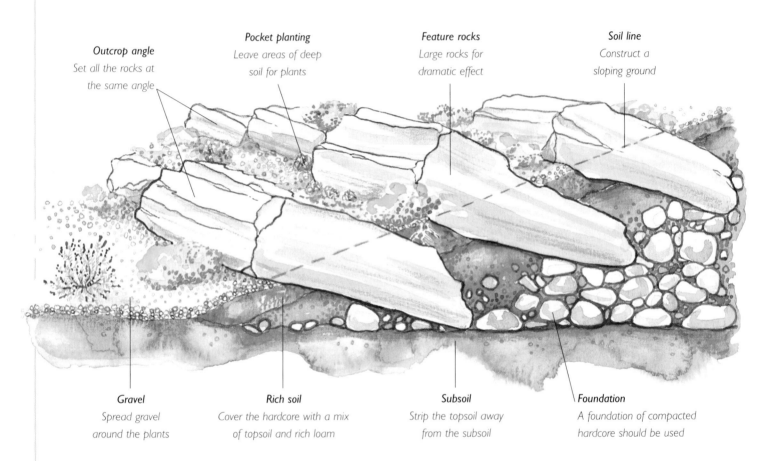

Outcrop angle
Set all the rocks at
the same angle

Pocket planting
Leave areas of deep
soil for plants

Feature rocks
Large rocks for
dramatic effect

Soil line
Construct a
sloping ground

Gravel
Spread gravel
around the plants

Rich soil
Cover the hardcore with a mix
of topsoil and rich loam

Subsoil
Strip the topsoil away
from the subsoil

Foundation
A foundation of compacted
hardcore should be used

Rockery design

A good rockery looks as if it is just the tip of a massive outcrop of stone that is hidden away under the ground. Do not attempt to build a rockery from hand-sized stones, arranging them haphazardly in an unlikely position, such as close to a lush border or round a swimming pool. It is much better to use a small number of large, well-weathered feature rocks, and to site them so that they rear up through an otherwise controlled area, such as a gravel bed or lawn.

Stone groups

Groups of rocks or large stones are sometimes likened to families, and through the centuries, they have often inspired folk tales. When these large rocks are set together in an otherwise rock-free landscape, they seem to invite questions and attention, and

cannot easily be ignored. Try this out for yourself on a slightly smaller scale, by grouping three big stones together on your lawn. Family, friends and neighbours will be sure to comment.

Standing guardians

Many societies have a tradition of erecting lone standing stones, for example the Japanese, the Chinese, and the Celts of ancient Britain. In the form of a monolithic slab set in the ground, such stones are almost invariably thought of as being guardians or sentinels. They are used to represent power, strength, permanence and dignity. If you want something similar in your own garden, the only problem with stones of this size is how to move them into position. If you have not got access to a tractor and hoist, ask a dozen or so friends to help, and move the stones with ropes, planks and rollers, a metal tube A-frame and a car winch.

OTHER TYPES OF ROCK GARDEN

Gravel and stone garden

A gravel and stone garden can be formal, with low walls, a tight pattern of stones, and a bed of gravel to cover the ground. Alternatively, it can be informal, with a natural spread of stones, and graded gravel to suggest a riverbed or scree. Start by planning out the paths, then cover the site with woven plastic sheet (to prevent weeds growing but allow drainage). Arrange a few good-size stones, then spread rivers of graded gravel and grit.

Grass and stone garden

To create a grass and stone garden, set three or four large stones (like islands) in a cropped lawn. Try various groupings for the stones and then, when you are happy with the layout, experiment by leaving selected areas of grass uncut. If there are wild meadow flowers growing in the long grass, and perhaps a sheltered space to sit in, or a flat slab of stone for a table, so much the better.

Pit and stone garden

One of the joys of walking in the country is coming across a secret, quiet place, that nobody else seems to know about. We once found a little dell, with a circle of rocks, several grassy mounds, and a sunken area in between. The dell appeared to be the site of something that had fallen into decay. Perhaps it was once an old house, an ancient village, or a well.

You can achieve a similar effect by digging a shallow hole in the lawn, grassing over the resulting mounds of soil, and grouping a few feature stones around the site.

ABOVE A gravel and stone garden. Spread the gravel so that it flows around the larger stones like a riverbed.

ABOVE Grass and stone garden. Let the grass around the stones grow long and mow a passageway between the mounds.

PLANTING A ROCKERY

Rock plants need a soil made up of one part fine gravel or grit, one part sand, and one part garden loam. Assess your soil to see whether it is alkaline or acidic, and purchase plants accordingly. For lime-loving rockery plants, use this basic soil mix, and scatter handfuls of flaked limestone about the site. Acid-loving plants will appreciate the addition of finely chopped bark instead.

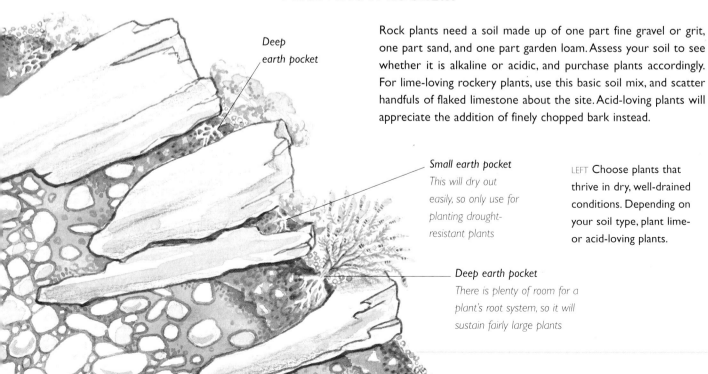

Deep earth pocket

Small earth pocket
This will dry out easily, so only use for planting drought-resistant plants

LEFT Choose plants that thrive in dry, well-drained conditions. Depending on your soil type, plant lime- or acid-loving plants.

Deep earth pocket
There is plenty of room for a plant's root system, so it will sustain fairly large plants

Walls and other structures

An old proverb says, "A wall without a gate is a prison, while a wall with a gate is a paradise". Building a stone wall is a wonderfully creative and fulfilling experience: one moment you have a space and the next you have a structure! It may be a practical wall to keep the children in, or a grand wall to make a statement.

DIFFERENT TYPES OF WALL

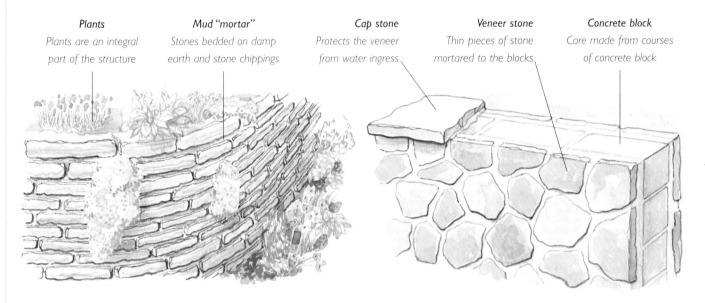

Plants
Plants are an integral part of the structure

Mud "mortar"
Stones bedded on damp earth and stone chippings

Cap stone
Protects the veneer from water ingress

Veneer stone
Thin pieces of stone mortared to the blocks

Concrete block
Core made from courses of concrete block

ABOVE Dry-stone retaining wall. The horizontal courses must be kept in line and the vertical joints staggered. The plants help bond the wall together because the roots run back into the retained soil.

ABOVE Veneered wall. Stones are arranged in a pattern that fits together well, and bedded in mortar. The stones are fixed one line at a time, leaving the mortar to stiffen before the next line is started.

Dry-stone walls

Dry-stone walls are traditionally made from whatever stone happens to be around, such as fieldstone, stone from the local quarry, or stone from a riverbed. Dry-stone walls always look at home in their surroundings for the simple reason that their colour and texture blends with the landscape in which they are found. In cross-section, dry-stone walls always taper in from a wide base, with low walls sitting directly on the ground, and high walls starting in a trench well below frost level. The walls may be topped off with coping stones on edge, stones laid flat, a layer of concrete and cobbles, or even a mix of stones, loose earth and turf.

Retaining walls

A retaining wall is best defined as a low wall that is used to hold back earth. Such walls are usually built on a sloping site where there is a need to step the ground to make a terrace. If you want to terrace a steep slope, it is better to go for a series of low walls rather than one or two high ones. Where the earth is heavy and wet, the

---

CAUTION

Make sure that all stone structures are strong, stable and adequately reinforced. Until you are experienced, don't attempt to build structures that are higher than head-height.

---

foundation is created in a deep trench, the wall is made extra wide at the foot, and as much rock spoil as possible is heaped behind the wall to supply extra drainage.

Mortared walls

Mortared walls are usually built on a concrete foundation. The courses are made from "ashlar" (cut and shaped stone) or rubble (uncut fieldstone). However, many mortared walls are made from salvaged cut stone and carefully selected fieldstone. There are four rules for building this type of wall: always rake back the mortar to reveal as much of the stone as possible, use a mortar that contains a good proportion of lime, make sure the mortar is stiff, and always wet the stone just before bonding. If you have any concerns about your wall-building project, such as getting the proportions of the mortar mix right, finding the colour or absorption rate of your chosen stone, deciding on the depth of the courses or the precise siting of the wall in the garden, it is a good idea to start off by building a small trial section of wall.

HOW TO BUILD A STRAIGHT WALL

Building procedure

1 Dig a trench to a depth of between 200–300 mm and lay a foundation of compacted rubble, topped with concrete (see page 24). Use a spirit level at all stages to ensure that everything is level.

2 Lay a course of stones, selecting and cutting stones to achieve best fit, for the whole length of the wall. Do your best to make sure that the stones are all of more or less equal thickness.

3 Put the stones carefully to one side, wet them and spread a generous layer of mortar over the foundation slab. Bed the stones in place on the mortar, and tap them down with the hammer. Make sure that the second course is well staggered against the first.

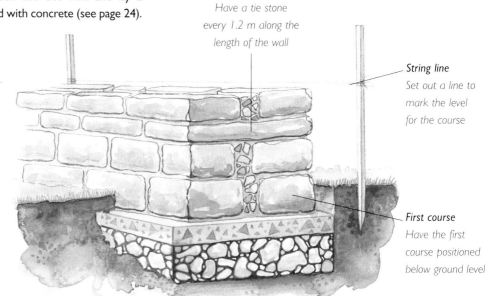

Tie stones
Have a tie stone every 1.2 m along the length of the wall

String line
Set out a line to mark the level for the course

First course
Have the first course positioned below ground level

PILLARS AND PIERS

Building a pillar

The techniques for building piers, square-section pillars and round-section pillars are similar. Building a round-section pillar, however, is a wonderful, skill-stretching experience that should not be missed. You are forever doing your best to fit the individual stones so that they run as close as possible to the circular section plan. It is best to practise laying a course of stones without mortar

first of all (all the stones that fit the edge of the circle, and then all the stones to fill in). Next put them to one side, spread the mortar, and bed the selected and trimmed stones in place. Tap down the whole layer of stones with a trowel or hammer, check the horizontal and vertical truth with a spirit level and make adjustments, then move on to the next course. If the courses bulge, stop building until the mortar has cured.

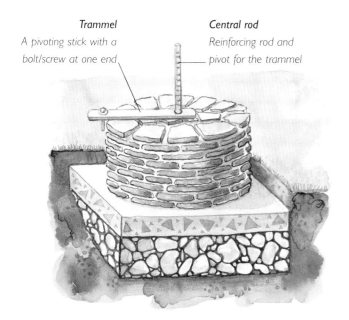

Trammel
A pivoting stick with a bolt/screw at one end

Central rod
Reinforcing rod and pivot for the trammel

ABOVE This method of building a round pillar uses a central rod and a trammel (a stick that is rotated to check the circumference).

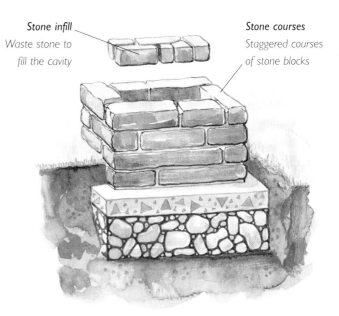

Stone infill
Waste stone to fill the cavity

Stone courses
Staggered courses of stone blocks

ABOVE A square stone pier. Courses are established and then infilled with waste stone. All the vertical joints are staggered.

Part 2: **Projects**

Stepping-stone path

Rough-cut stepping stones make a delightful path, which is perfect for light foot traffic, great for children playing jumping games, and also suitable for pushing a wheelbarrow on. The flow of stones meandering across the lawn fulfils a design function too, beautifully leading the eye from one garden feature to another.

TIME
About half a day (for nine medium-size stones).

SAFETY
Setting the stones is a difficult, finger-nipping task, so make sure that you wear thick leather gloves.

YOU WILL NEED

Materials *for a path with nine stepping stones*
- Flagstones: 9 salvaged slate or limestone flags about 500 mm long, 400 mm wide and 50 mm thick
- Soft sand: about 1 bucket of sand per stone

Tools
- Wheelbarrow
- Spade
- Fork
- Bucket
- Wooden tamping beam: about 500 mm long, 60 mm wide and 50 mm thick
- Sledgehammer

SITING THE PATH

Before you decide where to put the path, think about the ebb and flow of traffic in the garden. Work out how many times, during your day-to-day activities, you walk from one point to another. For example, when you empty the kitchen waste on to the compost heap, do you always take the same route? Do you avoid certain routes because the ground is muddy? Are there any worn areas on the lawn, which indicate heavy wear? They will be dusty and bald in summer, muddy and dipped in winter.

When you have considered all the options and variables, map out the best route for the path. Before you calculate the number of stones and their spacing, take into account the length of stride of the people most likely to use the path. Have a trial "stepping out" across the lawn to work out the required spacing. When you come to choosing the stones, it does not matter if they are different sizes and odd shapes, or even if there are great variations in thickness, as long as each stone has one sound, level face.

CROSS-SECTION THROUGH PATH

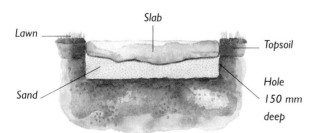

Lawn
Slab
Topsoil
Sand
Hole 150 mm deep

PLAN VIEW OF PATH

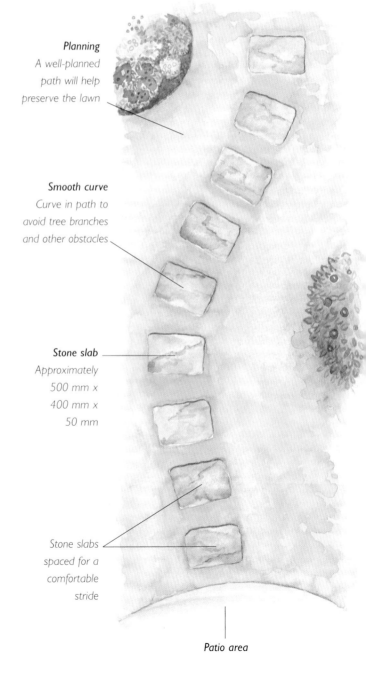

Planning
A well-planned path will help preserve the lawn

Smooth curve
Curve in path to avoid tree branches and other obstacles

Stone slab
Approximately 500 mm x 400 mm x 50 mm

Stone slabs spaced for a comfortable stride

Patio area

Step-by-step: **Making the stepping-stone path**

Spacing
Check that the spacing suits your length of stride

Best face
Make sure that the best face of the flagstone is uppermost

1 Set out the flagstones on the lawn, spacing them to suit the stride of the people who will use the path. Experiment with various alignments – curved, straight, or winding – until you are pleased with the overall effect. Arrange the individual flags so that the best face is uppermost.

Helpful hint

If, when you're putting the stones down, you notice that any are starting to delaminate slightly with handling, it is a sign that the stone is not very stable, and would wear rapidly. Reject it and replace with another.

Alignment
Adjust the flagstones so that they are aligned with each other

Lifting turf
A round-pronged fork is good for this

Depth
Aim for a recess about 150 mm deep

Turf
Only pick up as much turf as you can lift comfortably

2 Use a small, clean, sharp spade to cut into the ground around each stone. Hold the spade upright and cut to a depth of about 200 mm, making sure that the cuts cross over at the corners. Repeat this procedure for all the stones in the line.

3 Carefully lift the stone to one side. Quarter the defined turf with the spade, and use the fork to lift the quarters into the wheelbarrow. Take to the compost heap. With the spade, excavate the recess to an overall depth of about 150 mm.

Hole depth
Make adjustments to holes to
suit varying thicknesses of stone

Stone height
The stone needs to be
10 mm lower than the lawn

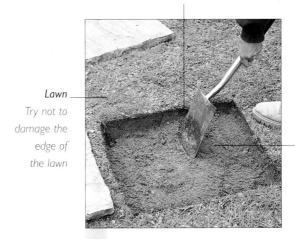

Corners
Clean the
earth from
the corners of
the holes

Lawn
Try not to
damage the
edge of
the lawn

Sand
Spread sand
over the recess

4 Work along the line of flagstones, removing the turf and soil, until you have a line of holes that fit the stones. Pay particular attention to the corners of the holes – they need to be crisp and clean.

5 Gauge the thickness of the stone and the depth of the hole, spread sand to a depth of 80–90 mm, then bed the stone in place. (Lift the stone and adjust the sand until the flagstone is about 10 mm lower than the lawn.)

Sledgehammer
Let the shaft of the hammer
slide through your hands

6 When the flagstone is nicely bedded on the sand, place the wooden beam diagonally across it and use the sledgehammer to gently tamp the stone into place. If the stone tilts or sinks, simply lift one edge and adjust the level of the sand.

Footwork
Hold the beam
secure with
your feet

Depth
If the slab does
not sit level,
remove it and
adjust the sand
underneath

Cobble spiral

Cobbles set in concrete make a great decorative feature, which can be employed to direct the movement of cars on your drive. The spaced cobbles are slightly uncomfortable to drive over, so visitors will instinctively steer round them. If you would like to enhance your drive with a feature that is attractive, hard-wearing and functional, cobbles are wonderfully suitable.

<table>
<tr><td>

TIME

A day to build, seven days for the concrete to cure.
</td></tr>
<tr><td>

SAFETY

Don't strain your back trying to lift a whole bag of cobbles. It is much better to open the bag and take out a few at a time.
</td></tr>
</table>

YOU WILL NEED

Materials *for a circle 1.8 m in diameter*
- Hardcore: 3 wheelbarrow loads broken rubble or stone
- Concrete: 1 part (50 kg) cement, 2 parts (100 kg) sharp sand, 3 parts (150 kg) aggregate
- Cobbles: 50 kg × 80 mm cobbles (allows for choice)
- Shingle: 25 kg × 25 mm shingle (allows for choice)

Tools
- Tape measure and chalk
- Wheelbarrow
- Sledgehammer
- Mason's hammer
- Spade and shovel
- Bucket
- Wooden tamping beam: about 900 mm long, 100 mm wide and 20 mm thick
- Bricklayer's trowel

MARKING AND PLANNING

Decide on the size of the circle according to your drive. Our circle has been made in an old flowerbed with an existing brick edging, but you could make a larger circle with a cobble edging (the radius of the circle should be no larger than you can reach).

Wash the cobbles, grade them from large to small, and have a trial dry-run. With tape measure and chalk, mark out a circle on the drive, pinpointing the centre. Transporting the cobbles in the wheelbarrow, position the biggest and best cobble at the centre. Add further stones to make a spiral, working clockwise, and finishing up with the smallest cobbles. Once the cobbles are in place, use the shingle to run a secondary spiral within the first.

We have increased the overall dynamic effect of the spiral by tamping the concrete to make a pattern that radiates out from the centre. Once the concrete has been mixed, you have to work at speed before it sets. Finally, don't forget to place a barrier around the finished circle so that you don't drive over it by mistake while it is drying.

PLAN VIEW OF THE COBBLE SPIRAL

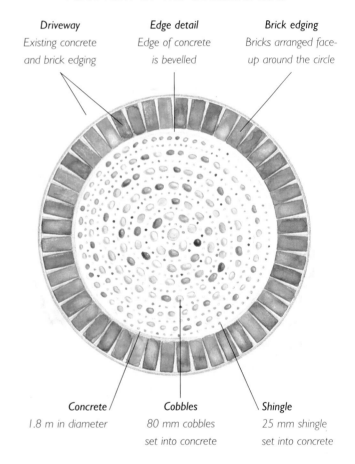

Driveway
Existing concrete and brick edging

Edge detail
Edge of concrete is bevelled

Brick edging
Bricks arranged face-up around the circle

Concrete
1.8 m in diameter

Cobbles
80 mm cobbles set into concrete

Shingle
25 mm shingle set into concrete

CROSS-SECTION DETAIL

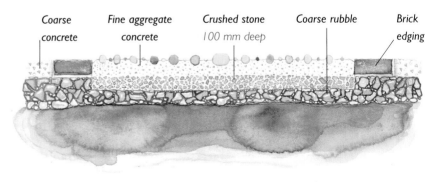

Coarse concrete

Fine aggregate concrete

Crushed stone
100 mm deep

Coarse rubble

Brick edging

Step-by-step: **Making the cobble spiral**

Hardcore
Pound the hardcore in place with the sledgehammer

Brick edge
Be careful not to damage any existing edging

 Having marked out the circle, dig it out to a depth of about 180 mm. (If you need to break up the concrete of the existing drive, use the sledgehammer and mason's hammer to do so.) Shovel in the hardcore and use the sledgehammer to pound it into place. The hardcore layer should be 100 mm deep.

Tamping
Work with a rapid tapping action

Pivot
Pivot one end of the beam on the centre point

Radial pattern
Tamp the concrete into a radial pattern

2 Measure out the dry ingredients that go to make the concrete (cement, sharp sand and aggregate). Fill the bucket with water. Mix sufficient water into the dry ingredients to make the correct consistency of concrete. Shovel the concrete into place, then use the beam to bring it to the same level as the brick edging and tamp it into a radial pattern.

Trowel angle
Angle the trowel into the brick edge

Smooth finish
Run the trowel around until the concrete is smooth

3 Holding the bricklayer's trowel at a sharp angle, run it around the edge of the concrete. Do this a couple of times, to achieve a smooth, bevelled finish.

Cobbles
Grade the cobbles into sizes

Spiral
Arrange the stones into a smooth spiral shape

Tapping
Allow the weight of the sledgehammer to fall on the cobble

4 Select a good cobble for the centre and use the weight of the sledgehammer to tap it very gently into place. Repeat the procedure with a dozen stones, establishing the pattern.

Damaged cobbles
Put damaged cobbles to
one side and avoid using

5 Continue setting out the cobbles, making sure they are aligned and then tamping them into place with the sledgehammer. Stand back periodically to check that the spiral relates evenly to the circle.

Trial placing
Set out about six cobbles at a time. Check for size and fit before you tap them into place

Spacing
Try to keep the spacing between the lines consistent

6 When you have placed all the cobbles, use the shingle to run a second spiral within the first. Use the mason's hammer to tap the pebbles into position. Leave the concrete to cure for seven days before driving on it.

Shingle
Run the line of shingle between the big cobbles

Helpful hint

Wash individual stones in water and set out a sequence of six or so stones at a time. Don't strike the stone, but rather let the weight of the hammer do most of the work. Continue gently tapping until the stone is slightly more than half buried in the concrete.

Natural outcrop rockery

A swift and easy way to add a dynamic feature to an otherwise level expanse of lawn is to build a rockery that looks like a natural outcrop. Rocks breaking through the ground suggest that there are powerful dynamic forces at work within the garden, while the well-drained environment allows you to cultivate a broad range of plants that enjoy these conditions.

YOU WILL NEED

Materials *for a rockery 3 m x 2.4 m x 600 mm*
- Soil: 1 tonne (5 parts good-quality topsoil to 1 part sharp sand)
- Feature rocks: 6 large sandstone rocks (the biggest you are able to move)
- Split sandstone: approximately 1 tonne (for foundation stones and decorative edging)
- Secondary rocks: 6 medium-sized sandstone rocks

- Alpine grit: 25 kg crushed granite
- Oyster shell grit: 25 kg well-washed crushed shell

Tools
- Fork
- Wheelbarrow
- Spade
- Club hammer
- Gardening trowel

A ROCK AND HEATHER MIX

Study the garden and think about the various options for the positioning of the rockery. Do you want to have a rockery island surrounded by a sea of lawn, or are you going to build it as a peninsular feature that divides two areas of lawn? Are you going to buy in the topsoil and build the rockery as a self-contained feature, or are you going to use earth moved from another project? (If you can use earth left over from another project, such as a pond excavation, or the topsoil removed prior to building an extension to the house, you save both time and money.)

The task of moving the rocks and earth is a major part of this project. Ideally, you need to plan the whole operation so that they only have to be shifted a short distance. Use a wheelbarrow and ask a friend to help you manoeuvre heavy rocks (see page 21).

It is preferable to choose a site for the rockery that is well away from formal borders, so that it does not create an imbalance between the various plantings in the garden. When we designed this rockery, we had in mind the sort of natural outcrop that you often see at the bottom of scree slopes, where rock and heather meet green pasture.

PLAN VIEW OF THE ROCKERY

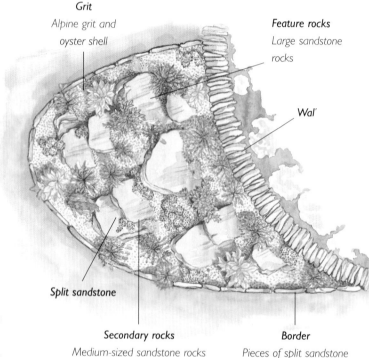

Grit
Alpine grit and oyster shell

Feature rocks
Large sandstone rocks

Wall

Split sandstone

Secondary rocks
Medium-sized sandstone rocks

Border
Pieces of split sandstone

CROSS-SECTION OF THE ROCKERY

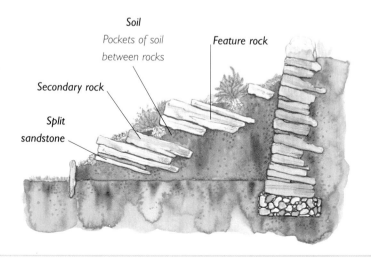

Soil
Pockets of soil between rocks

Feature rock

Secondary rock

Split sandstone

Step-by-step: Making the natural outcrop rockery

Retaining wall
Use an existing feature
as a retaining wall

Pocket slope
Angle the hole so that it
is deepest at the back

Spreading soil
Work the earth
with the fork
and your feet

Pocket
Dig a pocket
to match the
size of the
stone

Trial fit
You may need
several
attempts to get
the stone to fit
the hole

1 With the fork, work the mound of earth to remove weeds, lumps of clay and unwanted stones. Walk back and forth over the earth to collapse cavities and compact it into shape.

2 Load stones into the wheelbarrow and move them to the site. The large stones are grouped like a series of steps. Dig a pocket towards the bottom of the mound and carefully ease one of the largest feature stones into place.

Earth anchor
Load earth on the tail
end of the stone

Wedging
Compact the
earth so the
front of the
stone rears up.
Wedge waste
stone under
the front of
the rock
to preserve
the angle

3 When you are pleased with the overall position and angle of the feature stone, take some pieces of split sandstone and use the club hammer to bang them under the stone. The sandstone will wedge the feature stone firmly in place.

Helpful hint

Compact the earth under the leading edge of the stone until the stone is rearing up at the front with the bulk of its weight at the tail end. Add fragments of waste stone (or old bricks, concrete, or hardcore) to the compacted earth.

Secondary stones
Use smaller stones to
complement the arrangement

Soil
Soil incorporates grit
for drainage

Stone angle
Trowel earth
under the
stone to adjust
the angle

Outcrop angle
The stones
should rear
up at the
same angle

Edging
Use stone on
edge to define
the rockery

4 Work up the slope repeating the
procedure, until you achieve a series
of steps that slope back slightly into the
mound. Trowel earth in and around the
stones to hold them in place.

5 When you have completed the basic
outcrop, with all the stones rearing
up at the same angle, dig a trench around
the mound and define it with an edging of
split sandstone. Plant the rockery.

Plant colour
Choose plants that have
different seasons of interest

6 Finally, when you have
completed your planting,
scatter handfuls of alpine grit
and crushed oyster shell in and
around the plants and stones, to
cover the earth and help give the
impression that the rockery is
part of a natural outcrop.

Watering
Water the
plants to settle
the roots

Alpine grit and oyster shell
The spread of grit and
oyster shell helps the earth
to retain moisture

Inspirations: Rockeries

The contrast between large stones and minute plants is uniquely beautiful. However, rockeries come in many shapes and sizes, from the austere sand and rock gardens of Japan, through to the little stone rockeries that characterized English suburban gardens in the 1920s and 1930s. Regardless of size, most rock gardens use stone and plants to suggest or replicate a natural setting. There are rock plants suitable for all situations, from exposed sites to crevices, and both sunny and shady positions.

RIGHT A flight of railway sleeper steps has been transformed into an eye-catching rockery simply by edging the steps with carefully chosen limestone rocks, spreading an infill of crushed stone between the wooden treads, and planting with species that thrive in a well-drained alkaline soil.

ABOVE A water rockery garden of Welsh slate planted with dwarf conifers and alpines. This rockery is reminiscent of high mountain passes, ice-cold springs and tranquillity.

RIGHT A Feng Shui rockery garden designed by Pamela Woods. Large feature rocks, gravel, wooden decking and water create a sublimely peaceful garden space.

Tessellated paving

An exciting and creative way of repairing an existing paved patio is to replace damaged slabs with an infill pattern of tessellated tiles. All you do is remove the slabs, revealing the underlying base, then bed in the tiles with a skim of mortar.

YOU WILL NEED

Materials *for 2 areas of paving 920 mm square*
- Mortar: 2 parts (30 kg) cement, 1 part (15 kg) lime, 9 parts (135 kg) soft sand
- Concrete tiles (imitation terracotta): 8 lozenge tiles (510 x 215 mm), 22 small square tiles (150 x 150 mm), 1 large square tile (300 x 300 mm)
- Shingle: 25 kg washed shingle (15–25 mm)

Tools
- Club hammer
- Wheelbarrow
- Tape measure and piece of chalk
- Bucket
- Spade and shovel
- Wooden tamping beam: about 400 mm long, 60 mm wide and 25 mm thick
- Mortar float
- Bricklayer's trowel

PRETTY AS A PICTURE

In this project, the word "tessellate" refers to the act of grouping tiles so that they fit together like a mosaic or a tiled floor. Identical square tiles tessellate to make a chequer-board pattern, but more dynamic effects can be obtained when two or more different shapes are arranged to create an overall repeat pattern, like the lozenge-shaped and square tiles in our two designs.

We lifted eight concrete slabs to create two identical square recesses. To remove a slab, hit it in the middle with a club hammer and pick the broken pieces out with a trowel. Note how we have used three shapes to fit the frame – a lozenge and two different squares – and then filled in around the tiles with a pattern of shingle. It is best to start with just a few shapes, playing around with various arrangements until you come up with an exciting design, and then to purchase additional tiles to suit your needs.

PLAN VIEW OF THE TESSELLATED PAVING

Shingle
Decorative shingle set in mortar

Small square tile
150 x 150 mm

Paved area
Existing paving slab surround

Large square tile
300 x 300 mm

Lozenge tile
510 x 215 mm

CROSS-SECTION OF THE TESSELLATED PAVING

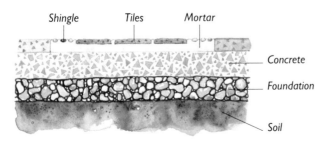

Shingle   Tiles   Mortar

Concrete

Foundation

Soil

Step-by-step: Making the tessellated paving

Existing slabs
Make sure existing slabs are stable

Corners
Make sure the mortar gets right into the corners

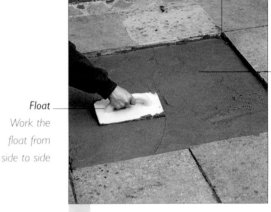

Tamping
Use a wooden beam to tamp the mortar level

Float
Work the float from side to side

Uniform bed
Aim for a smooth, level finish

1 Use the tape measure and chalk to draw guidelines on the concrete slabs. Sprinkle water over the exposed foundation, shovel the mortar into place, and tamp it level with the beam so that it ends up slightly lower than the slabs.

2 Use the mortar float to skim the mortar into the corners and right to the edges of the recess. Work the float from side to side to achieve a uniform bed with no cavities or bumps.

Centre-line
Make sure the tiles are aligned with the registration marks

3 One at a time, dip the tiles in a bucket of water, shake off the excess and then very carefully set them in position on the wet mortar. When the design is in place, use the handle of the bricklayer's trowel to tap and adjust the individual tiles.

Tapping
Use the handle of the trowel to tap the tile in position

Wet the tiles
In hot weather sprinkle water over the tiles to hold back the drying time of the mortar

Tile level
Keep the tiles level with
the surrounding slabs

4 If, at any point along the
way, a tile sinks too deeply
or sticks up at an angle, lift it
with the point of the trowel, add
a little more mortar, and then
gently bed it back into place.

Helpful hint

If the day is sunny and the
tiles feel hot and dry to the
touch, soak the back of
each tile in water just prior
to bedding it into the
mortar. Wiggle the tile
rapidly on the spot until
you feel it begin to settle.

Bedding
Move the tile
from side to
side to bed it
in place

5 Finally, when all the tiles are
in position, use the shingle
to make patterns in the remaining
areas of mortar. Set the pebbles
in one at a time. Leave for
24 hours before it is dry enough
for light traffic, or seven days
before it is ready for heavy use.

Shingle patterns
Arrange the
shingle into a
pleasing pattern

Cleaning
Use a damp
cloth to clean
the tiles and
remove spots
of mortar

Raised bed

A raised bed gives you the opportunity to add an extra planting area to your garden, and the change in level creates interest. You can build it on an existing patio or area of concrete. The good thing about raised beds is that you do not have to stoop to weed them. This one is built from double-sided reconstituted stone blocks.

TIME

A weekend to build (two full days to build on an existing patio base).

SAFETY

Reconstituted stone blocks are heavy and fragile. Handle the blocks with care, preferably wearing gloves.

YOU WILL NEED

Materials *for a bed 1.10 m square and 510 mm high*
- Mortar: 2 parts (20 kg) cement, 1 part (10 kg) lime, 9 parts (90 kg) soft sand
- Double-sided "York stone" blocks: 48 blocks, 450 mm long, 150 mm wide and 65 mm thick
- Straight "York stone" coping blocks: 8 blocks, 450 mm long, 185 mm wide and 47 mm thick

Tools
- Wheelbarrow
- Tape measure and piece of chalk
- Spirit level and a length of batten
- Shovel
- Bucket
- Bricklayer's trowel
- Mason's hammer
- Pointing trowel
- Stiff brush

A BED ON THE PATIO

If you are looking for a project that involves the minimum of effort and expertise, this is a good one to try. The sizes specified for the wall blocks and coping blocks allow you to build a rectilinear form without the need for cutting. The clever design of the blocks means that all the on-view faces are textured.

This project is designed to be set directly on to a base of existing patio slabs, avoiding the need to build a foundation. The bed can be sited away from walls, so that it can be viewed and approached from all sides, or it can back on to a wall. If you are going to put it near a building, make sure that there is enough space for you to move the blocks into position.

PLAN VIEW OF THE RAISED BED

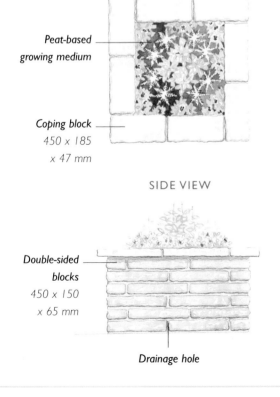

Peat-based growing medium

Coping block
450 x 185 x 47 mm

SIDE VIEW

Double-sided blocks
450 x 150 x 65 mm

Drainage hole

CROSS-SECTION OF THE RAISED BED

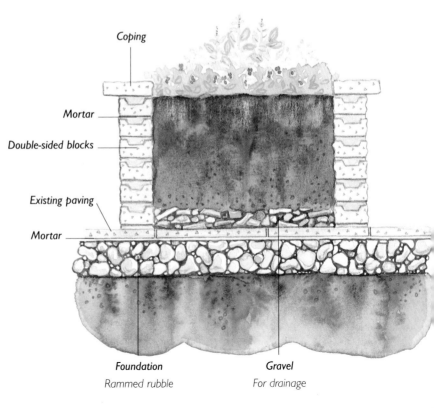

Coping

Mortar

Double-sided blocks

Existing paving

Mortar

Foundation
Rammed rubble

Gravel
For drainage

Step-by-step: **Making the raised bed**

Chalk lines
*Use the chalk to set
out guidelines*

Spirit level
*Check with
the spirit level
to see if the
blocks are
sitting level*

Drainage
*Leave one
vertical course
open on each
side of the first
course for a
drainage hole*

I Use the tape measure, chalk and spirit level to establish the position of the bed. Take eight wall blocks to form the first course of the bed. Arrange them in position so that each side of the bed shows two long faces of the blocks and one end face.

Helpful hint

When you come to testing with the spirit level, be aware that a vertical height difference of, say, 5 mm might be caused by no more than a blob of mortar. Wipe both the spirit level and the top of the blocks before taking a reading.

Buttering
*Butter the end of the
block with the mortar*

Mortar
*Do not worry about mortar
oozing out inside the bed*

Tapping
*Use the
hammer to
tap blocks
into line*

*Staggered
courses*
*Arrange the
courses so that
the blocks
overlap joins*

Mortar bed
*Lay down a
generous bed
of mortar*

2 Use the bricklayer's trowel to lay down a bed of mortar. Dampen the blocks and patio slabs. Place a block on the mortar, butter the end of the next block with mortar and set it alongside. Continue in the same way for all eight blocks.

3 Check that the blocks are level with the spirit level and the batten. Tap any blocks that stand proud with the mason's hammer. Repeat the procedure for the next course of blocks. Note how the pattern of blocks is staggered.

Sighting
Look down the wall and
tap blocks into position

Mortar
Clean the mortar off the top
before levelling

Checking
After each
course, check
that blocks
are level and
aligned

Levelling
Make sure that
both the batten
and the spirit
level are free
from blobs of
mortar

4 Continue laying one course of blocks upon another, all the while checking that they are horizontal with the spirit level and batten, tapping blocks into place with the mason's hammer, and tidying up the mortar with the pointing trowel.

5 When you have built all six courses, rake out some of the mortar with the pointing trowel. Clean up with the stiff brush and check the overall squareness of the structure by setting the spirit level across the corners. If you need to make adjustments, use the batten to tap blocks into place, rather than the spirit level.

Tapping
Use the trowel handle to tap
the blocks into final position

6 Finally, lay a bed of mortar on the top course and set the coping stones in place. Their back edge should be level with the inside face of the wall; the front edge forms a nosing or lip around the bed. Before filling the bed with soil, allow two days for the mortar to dry.

Bedding
Twist the block
slightly back
and forth while
applying light
pressure

Raking
Leave the raking
(scraping excess
mortar from
between the
blocks) until the
mortar is half-set

Flagstone steps

Flagstone steps are not only a practical and functional means of coping with a steep, sloping garden, but are also a dynamic design feature in their own right. The steps lead the eye from one level to another, and suggest that there are other exciting areas of garden still to be explored. This project consists of three steps.

TIME

A weekend to build three steps, seven days for the concrete and mortar to set before walking on the steps.

SPECIAL TIPS

The longer the concrete is kept moist during the curing (drying) process, the stronger it will be. Each day, for seven days, sprinkle the concrete with water. Keep the steps covered with plastic sheet, sacking or old carpet.

CROSS-SECTION OF THE FLAGSTONE STEPS

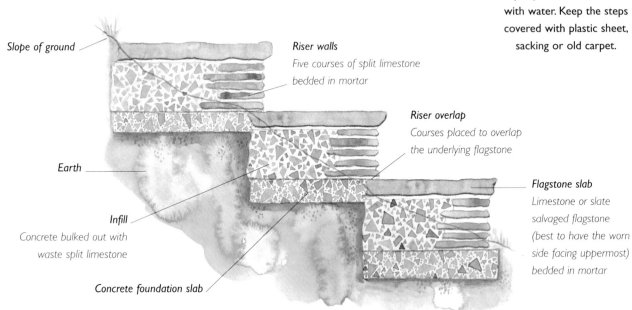

Slope of ground

Riser walls
Five courses of split limestone
bedded in mortar

Riser overlap
Courses placed to overlap
the underlying flagstone

Earth

Flagstone slab
Limestone or slate
salvaged flagstone
(best to have the worn
side facing uppermost)
bedded in mortar

Infill
Concrete bulked out with
waste split limestone

Concrete foundation slab

YOU WILL NEED

Materials *For 3 steps,
each 600 mm wide, 420 mm
deep and 170 mm high*
• Concrete: 1 part (40 kg)
  cement, 2 parts (80 kg)
  sharp sand, 3 parts
  (120 kg) aggregate
• Mortar: 2 parts (24 kg)
  cement, 1 part (12 kg) lime,
  9 parts (108 kg) soft sand
• Slate or limestone flagstones:
  3 salvaged flags, about
  600 mm long, 420 mm wide
  and 40 mm thick
• Split limestone: 3 square
  metres salvaged roof stone,
  about 15 mm thick

Tools
• Wheelbarrow
• Bucket
• Tape measure and a piece
  of chalk
• Spade and shovel
• Wooden beam for tamping:
  about 600 mm long, 80 mm
  wide and 50 mm thick
• Spirit level
• Mason's hammer
• Bricklayer's trowel
• Club hammer
• Pointing trowel

UP AND DOWN THE GARDEN

Study the site and visualize how the steps will relate to the overall layout of the garden – the slope of the land, other features within the garden, and underground structures, such as foundations and pipes. When the flagstones are in place, the treads measure no less than 420 mm from the edge of the step to the riser. The riser walls are about 125 mm high, to give a total step height of no more than 170 mm. Each step is constructed in four stages – laying the concrete foundation slab, building the riser wall, back-filling behind the riser wall, and setting the flagstone in place.

The concrete foundation slabs are made from a 1-2-3 mix – 1 part cement, 2 parts sharp sand and 3 parts aggregate, and the infill is bulked out with waste stone. The mortar is 2-1-9 mix – 2 parts cement, 1 part lime, and 9 parts soft sand. The riser walls are built from five courses of salvaged roof stone, with the best edges of the stone placed on view. Finally, while we have covered the cut-in ground at the sides of the steps with pieces of flint, you might prefer to use something different, such as gravel, found field-stone, turf, ground-cover plants or crushed bark.

Flagstone steps

FRONT VIEW OF THE FLAGSTONE STEPS, INCLUDING CROSS-SECTION DETAIL

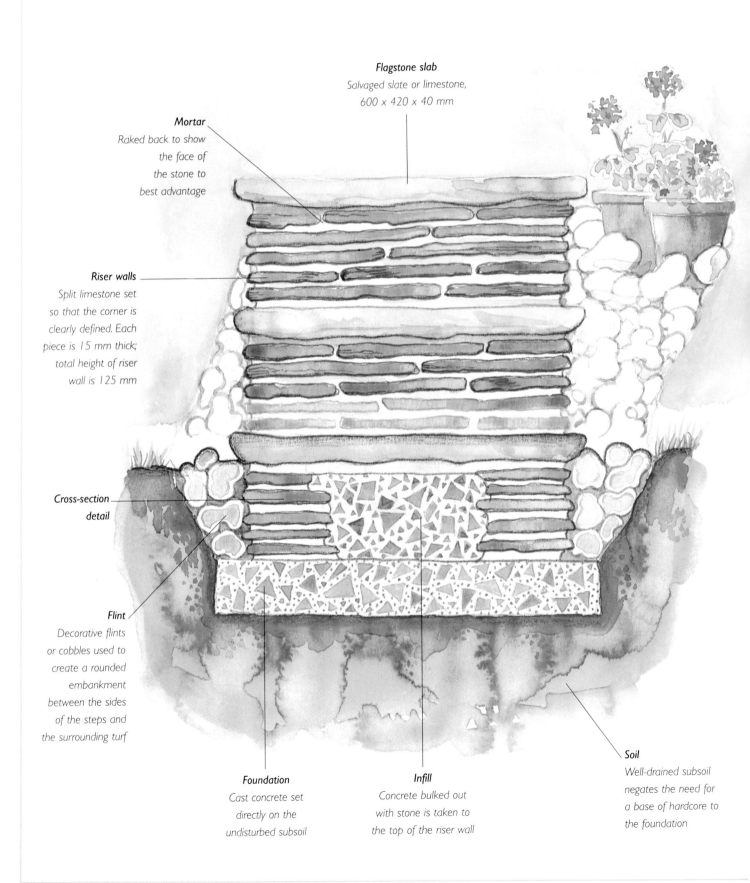

Flagstone slab
Salvaged slate or limestone,
600 x 420 x 40 mm

Mortar
Raked back to show
the face of
the stone to
best advantage

Riser walls
Split limestone set
so that the corner is
clearly defined. Each
piece is 15 mm thick;
total height of riser
wall is 125 mm

Cross-section
detail

Flint
Decorative flints
or cobbles used to
create a rounded
embankment
between the sides
of the steps and
the surrounding turf

Foundation
Cast concrete set
directly on the
undisturbed subsoil

Infill
Concrete bulked out
with stone is taken to
the top of the riser wall

Soil
Well-drained subsoil
negates the need for
a base of hardcore to
the foundation

PLAN VIEW OF THE FLAGSTONE STEPS

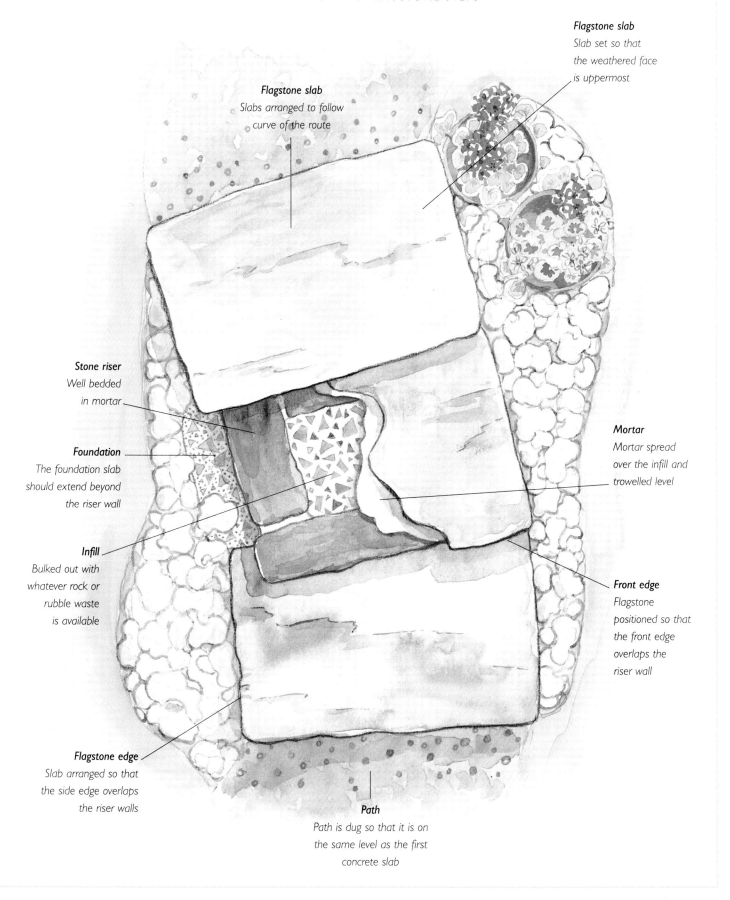

Flagstone slab
Slabs arranged to follow
curve of the route

Flagstone slab
Slab set so that
the weathered face
is uppermost

Stone riser
Well bedded
in mortar

Foundation
The foundation slab
should extend beyond
the riser wall

Infill
Bulked out with
whatever rock or
rubble waste
is available

Mortar
Mortar spread
over the infill and
trowelled level

Front edge
Flagstone
positioned so that
the front edge
overlaps the
riser wall

Flagstone edge
Slab arranged so that
the side edge overlaps
the riser walls

Path
Path is dug so that it is on
the same level as the first
concrete slab

Step-by-step: **Making the flagstone steps**

Trench
*Cut the trench so that
there is room to work*

Spoil
*Try to minimize the amount
of earth fall at this stage*

Tamping
*Tamp the
concrete level
with the
wooden beam*

Marking
*Draw around
the slab
with chalk*

Alignment
*Angle the
flagstone in the
direction of
the flight*

1 To build the first step, mark out the foundation trench with the tape measure, making it about 900 mm wide and 700 mm from front to back. Dig down to a depth of 100 mm. Fill the trench with concrete and tamp it down with the wooden beam. Check that it is level.

2 Leave the concrete foundation to harden overnight. Next, place a flagstone on the concrete, angling it in the direction of the flight, and mark the position with the chalk. Put the flagstone to one side.

Corners
*Keep the corners crisp
and square*

Trimming
*Trim the stone
for the best fit*

3 Allowing for the flagstone to overhang at the front and side edges by 10–20 mm, select pieces of limestone for the front and side walls of the riser. Trim them to size with the mason's hammer. Pay special attention to the construction of the front and corners of the riser, and make sure they are square.

Helpful hint

The more time that you spend at the dry-run stage – choosing and arranging the stones for best fit, and trimming edges to shape – the easier it will be when you come to bedding the stones on the mortar.

4 Build the box by bedding the five courses of split limestone in mortar, building to a height of 125 mm. Fill the cavity with concrete and waste stone, tamp down level with the beam, and leave to set. Use the bricklayer's trowel to butter a 30 mm-layer of mortar over the top of the step. Some of the mortar will ooze out when the flagstone is positioned.

Filling
Fill the cavity with concrete and waste stone

Levelling
Tamp the courses level with the beam

Positioning
Slowly lower the flagstone on to the bed of mortar

Horizontal check
Check the foundation with the spirit level

Adjustment
When the slab is in place, adjust it so that the front edge slopes down by 10 mm, so rain can run off

Tamping
Use the beam to tamp the concrete level

Concrete
The concrete foundation needs to be level with the flagstone

5 Carefully lower the flagstone into position. Tamp down with the club hammer and check it is level with the spirit level. Adjust the stone so that the front edge slopes down by 10 mm. Use the pointing trowel to tidy up the mortar.

6 To build the next step, dig another foundation cavity (the same size as the first cavity) behind the first step. Fill the cavity, build the riser walls and position the flagstone as previously described. Repeat the procedure for each new step.

Alpine hypertufa trough

In the 1940s, gardeners developed a technique for covering old glazed white kitchen sinks with a mixture of sphagnum moss, sand and cement to make them look like stone. It was called hypertufa, after tufa, the rock it ressembled, and became all the rage. This project takes the technique one step further, in that we cast a whole trough from hypertufa. The project rises up like magic from the ground!

TIME
Two weekends: two days to dig out the mould and for casting (five days for the hypertufa to cure), and two more days for digging out the trough.

SAFETY
This project involves a lot of strenuous digging and heaving – you will need a willing helper.

CROSS-SECTION OF THE TROUGH

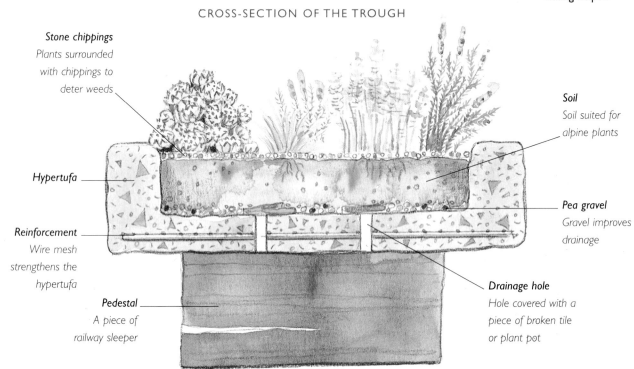

Stone chippings
Plants surrounded with chippings to deter weeds

Hypertufa

Reinforcement
Wire mesh strengthens the hypertufa

Pedestal
A piece of railway sleeper

Soil
Soil suited for alpine plants

Pea gravel
Gravel improves drainage

Drainage hole
Hole covered with a piece of broken tile or plant pot

YOU WILL NEED

Materials *for a trough 600 mm long, 400 mm wide and 130 mm high (not including height of pedestal)*
- Hypertufa mix: 25 kg cement, 25 kg sharp sand, 10 kg sphagnum moss
- Broomstick dowel: 2 x 150 mm long
- Wire grid mesh: 25 mm mesh, 570 mm long, 370 mm wide
- Railway sleeper: 400 mm long, 300 mm wide, 145 mm thick

Tools
- Spade and shovel
- Tape measure
- String line and 8 pegs
- Spirit level
- Sledgehammer
- Gardening trowel
- Mason's hammer
- Wheelbarrow and bucket
- Wooden tamping beam: about 600 mm long, 80 mm wide and 25 mm thick
- Wire clippers
- Pointing trowel
- Stiff brush

BURIED TREASURE

Find an area of rough, uncultivated ground in the garden for casting the trough – perhaps a corner of the vegetable plot, or a flower bed that is going to be grassed over. Ideally, you need an area that is reasonably well drained: a mix of heavy loam and clay (where you can squeeze a handful of the earth into a ball that holds its shape) would be perfect. If you study the working drawings and the photographs, you will see that the trough is cast upside-down, with a sheet of wire mesh used to reinforce the base. The drainage holes are created by the two dowels. The hollows and bumps in the ground are reversed to become bumps and holes in the trough or, to put it another way, the hollow of the trough starts out as a bump in the ground. The finished trough weighs about 150 kg, which might make it difficult to get out of the ground, so enlist the help of friends and family.

Alpine hypertufa trough

FRONT VIEW OF TROUGH

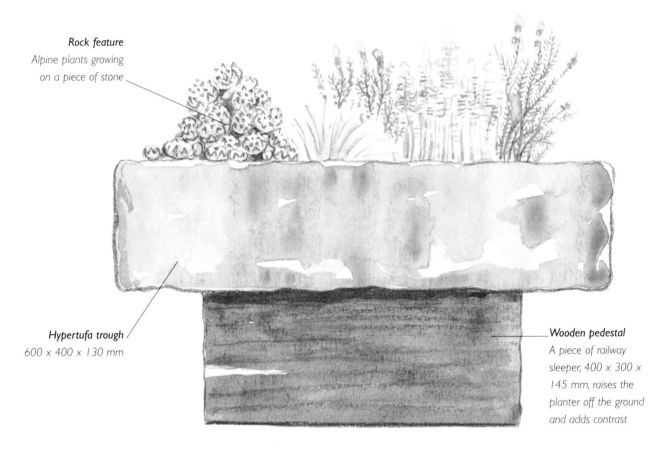

Rock feature
Alpine plants growing
on a piece of stone

Hypertufa trough
600 x 400 x 130 mm

Wooden pedestal
A piece of railway
sleeper, 400 x 300 x
145 mm, raises the
planter off the ground
and adds contrast

PLAN VIEW OF TROUGH

Sides of trough
Casting hypertufa in
earth produces a
rugged, stone-like finish

Strong sides
Sides are at least
70 mm thick

PLAN VIEW OF TROUGH DURING CASTING

Hypertufa
A final layer – smoothed and
levelled – covers the mesh

Reinforcement
Wire mesh is positioned within
the thickness of the base

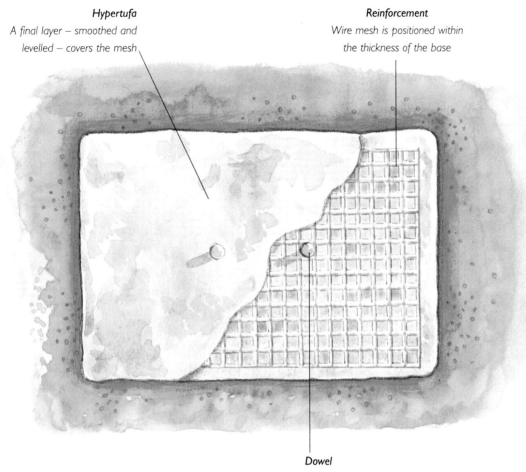

Dowel
Dowel inserted through the mesh and entire
thickness of the base (to create drainage holes)

CROSS-SECTION OF TROUGH DURING EXCAVATION

Excavation
A hole is dug
around the trough

Hypertufa

Dowel

Reinforcing mesh
Set approximately
half-way through
the 50 mm
thickness of the
trough base

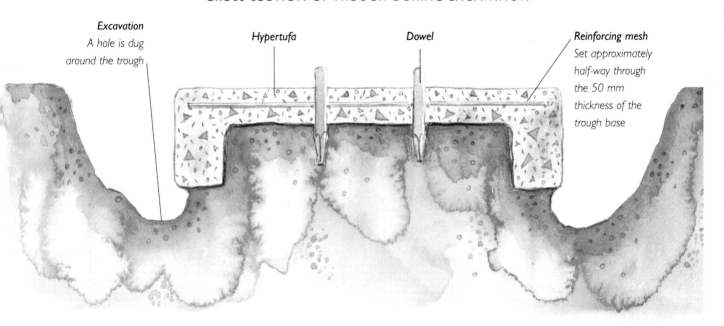

Step-by-step: Making the alpine hypertufa trough

Marking out
Set the shape out with
pegs and string

1 Clear the ground of weeds and stones, and skim it level with a spade. Use the tape measure, string and pegs to set out a rectangle about 600 mm long and 400 mm wide.

Helpful hint

The traditional method of using two pegs at the corners, with the strings crossing, not only allows you to set out the shape without damaging the earth at the corners, but it also means that you can leave the arrangement in place when you are excavating.

Corners
The position of
the pegs allows
the string to
cross over at
the corners

Level
Adjust the level of the
earth prior to pounding

Scoring
Use the point of the trowel
to score a guideline

Pounding
Pound the
earth to
a hard,
compacted
finish

Depth
Clean out the
earth to
a depth of
50 mm

Digging
Work with
small strokes
to keep the
edges crisp

2 Having pegged out the form and checked the overall level with the spirit level, take the sledgehammer and systematically pound the earth around the strings until it is hard and compact.

3 Following the line of the string, score the rectangle on the ground with the gardening trowel. Remove the pegs and string. Excavate the area to a depth of about 50 mm. Try and keep the sides of the excavation clean and sharp.

Trench width
*The trench needs to
be 70 mm wide*

Trench width
*The trench needs to
be 70 mm wide*

Trench depth
*Dig out the
trench to a total
depth of
130 mm*

4 Measure in 70 mm from
the sides of the hole and
then sink this area a further
80 mm. You should be left with an
upside-down trough shape, with a
total depth of 130 mm. Bang the
two dowels into the central base
with the mason's hammer. Mix up
the hypertufa by adding water to
the cement, sharp sand and moss.
It should resemble porridge.

Dowels
*Be careful you do
not break up the
earth when you
hammer in
the dowels*

Wire mesh
*If necessary, trim the mesh
to fit over the two pegs*

Curing
*The water improves
the curing process*

Tamping
*Top up the
hypertufa so it
is level with the
ground and
tamp down*

Holes
*The drainage
holes run
right through
the base*

Cleaning
*Scrub off all
traces of earth
using a brush*

5 Fill the excavation with hypertufa to
within 25 mm of the surface, and
tamp it level with the beam. Cut the mesh
with the clippers and fit it over the pegs.
Top up the mix to ground level and tamp
down. Smooth off with the pointing trowel.

6 Wait about five days for the
hypertufa to cure, then carefully
excavate the trough. Ease out the two pegs
and use a stiff brush and running water to
remove all traces of loose earth. Sit the
finished trough on the railway sleeper.

Inspirations: Troughs and planters

Nothing beats troughs and planters for versatility in the garden. They can be filled with eye-catching displays at any time of year, giving you the opportunity to make the most of what is in season. Many objects can be used as containers, ranging from a classic lead cistern from a grand house, to a stone drinking trough for animals, an old sink, or a modern reconstituted stone or wooden trough.

ABOVE **A** classic trough hosts a flourish of *Helichrysum petiolare*, pelargoniums and various seedlings. The trough neatly indicates that the door is not in use. The plants have all been left in their pots so that the display can be changed easily.

RIGHT **A** simple stone trough contrasts beautifully with the traditional brickwork of the walls and the bold ceramic pot alongside. The planting themes of the two containers echo each other, visually linking two rather different objects together.

FAR RIGHT **An** ancient stone trough, planted with *Aubretia deltoidea*, mounted on a stone pedestal. It is thought by the owner that both the trough and the base are ecclesiastical – perhaps a font with a piece of broken capital for the base.

Paved circle

The wonderful thing about a paved circle is that it immediately becomes a focus point in the garden. Children enjoy playing hop, skip and jump games on the pattern of stones, it is a good surface for bench seats and tables, and it makes a really great barbecue area. This design is about 2.5 m in diameter, but make it bigger if desired.

CROSS-SECTION OF HALF OF THE PAVED CIRCLE

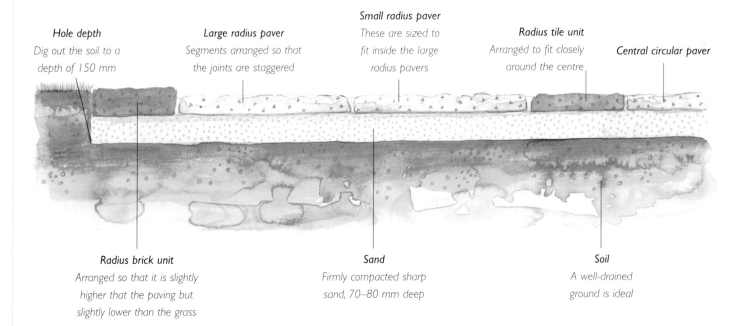

Hole depth
Dig out the soil to a depth of 150 mm

Large radius paver
Segments arranged so that the joints are staggered

Small radius paver
These are sized to fit inside the large radius pavers

Radius tile unit
Arranged to fit closely around the centre

Central circular paver

Radius brick unit
Arranged so that it is slightly higher that the paving but slightly lower than the grass

Sand
Firmly compacted sharp sand, 70–80 mm deep

Soil
A well-drained ground is ideal

YOU WILL NEED

Materials *for a circle 2.54 m in diameter*
- Central circular paver: 450 mm in diameter
- Radius tile units: 4 x 235 mm (inside radius)
- Small radius pavers: 16 x 485 mm (inside radius)
- Large radius pavers: 16 x 675 mm (inside radius)
- Radius brick units: 16 x 1.04 m (inside radius)
- Sharp sand: 500 kg
- Lime: 50 kg

Tools
- Wheelbarrow
- Tape measure
- String line
- Spade
- Fork
- Rake
- Heavy wooden mallet
- Wooden tamping beam: about 500 mm long, 60 mm wide and 50 mm thick
- Spirit level
- Bass broom

MAGIC CIRCLES

Wander around your garden to work out the best place for a circle that is about 2.5 m in diameter. It could be under a tree, which would make a nice shaded area for a bench seat and table, or in a central position to make a feature, perhaps with a sundial. Study the garden in terms of adequate drainage, shade, sun, and flow of traffic, and assess the pros and cons of the options.

When you have decided on a possible site, make sure that the area is free from underground pipes and drain covers. If you have the plans for your property, pipes may be marked; if not, dig very carefully. Use the string line to scribe a circle to size, and then stand back to see how it fits in with the garden. As a further check, to make sure that you like the position of the circle before committing to construction, set out the slabs and leave them in place for a couple of days. Note how the circle relates to the sun and shade throughout the day. When you are satisfied with the position, chop around the circle with the spade, remove the paving slabs to a safe place, and the work can begin.

Paved circle

PLAN VIEW OF HALF OF THE PAVED CIRCLE

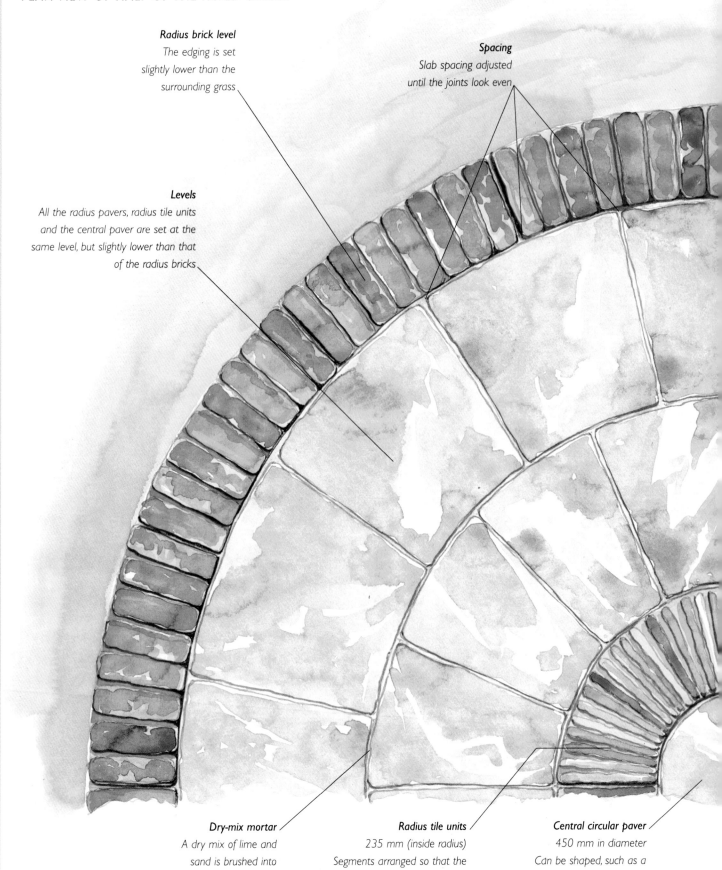

Radius brick level
The edging is set
slightly lower than the
surrounding grass

Spacing
Slab spacing adjusted
until the joints look even

Levels
All the radius pavers, radius tile units
and the central paver are set at the
same level, but slightly lower than that
of the radius bricks

Dry-mix mortar
A dry mix of lime and
sand is brushed into
the joints

Radius tile units
235 mm (inside radius)
Segments arranged so that the
radial joints are equally spaced

Central circular paver
450 mm in diameter
Can be shaped, such as a
millstone, or made of bricks

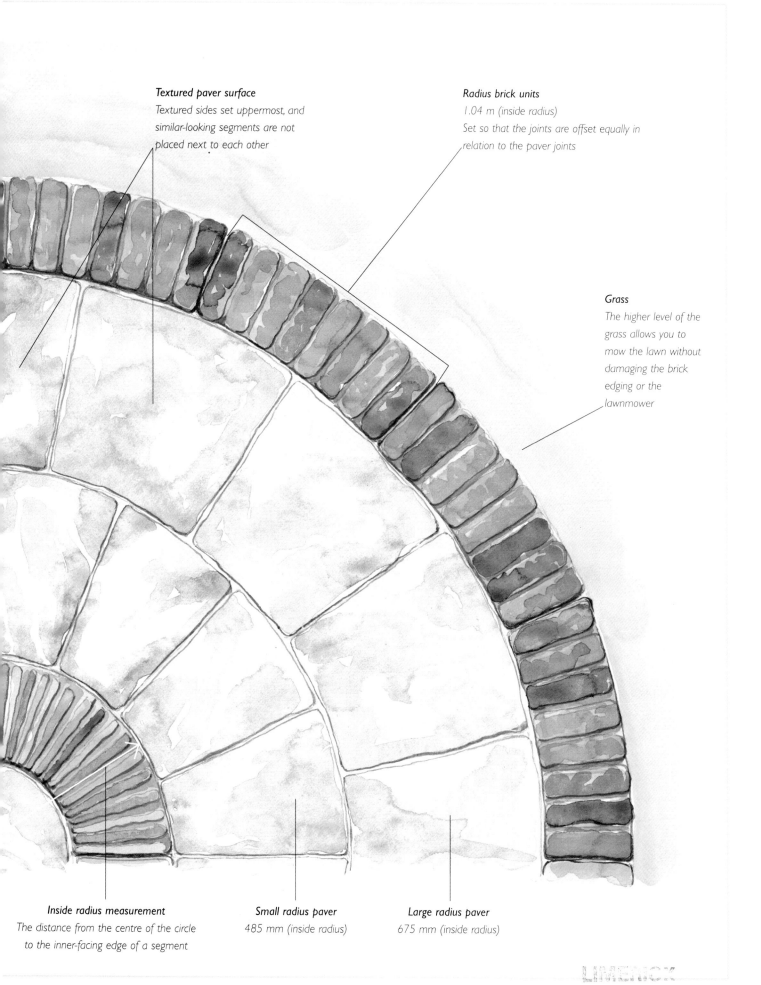

Textured paver surface
Textured sides set uppermost, and
similar-looking segments are not
placed next to each other

Radius brick units
1.04 m (inside radius)
Set so that the joints are offset equally in
relation to the paver joints

Grass
The higher level of the
grass allows you to
mow the lawn without
damaging the brick
edging or the
lawnmower

Inside radius measurement
The distance from the centre of the circle
to the inner-facing edge of a segment

Small radius paver
485 mm (inside radius)

Large radius paver
675 mm (inside radius)

Step-by-step: **Making the paved circle**

Earth
Dig out the earth to a
depth of 150 mm

Circle centre
The intersection of the
arcs marks the centre

Stones
Remove any
rubble and
big stones

Raking
Rake the
sand level
and smooth

Compacting
Do not worry
about walking
on the sand

1 Use the spade and fork to remove all the turf and earth from the marked area down to a depth of about 150 mm, and rake the earth level. Cover the area with a layer of sand to a depth of 70–80 mm, and rake it smooth and level.

2 To find the centre of the circle, use the string line. Set it to measure the radius of the circle, then spike the line at a couple of points around the circumference and strike arcs. The intersection of the arcs is the centre of the circle.

Tamping
Hit the beam with the mallet
rather than hitting the slab

3 Put the circular slab at the centre and tamp it in place with the mallet and wooden beam. Check with the spirit level and make corrections until the slab lies absolutely level.

*Horizontal
check*
Make sure the
slab is
positioned
correctly using
the spirit level

Levelling
You might need
to pack sand
under the slab to
adjust the level

Segments
Handle fragile segments
with great care

Packing
A dipped
slab needs to
be raised with
extra sand
underneath

4 Working outwards from the centre, carefully position the other slabs (the circle of radius tile units, the circle of small radius pavers, and so on), all the while checking with the spirit level and correcting any dips and hollows with extra sand.

Helpful hint

If you experience difficulties when you come to spacing the slabs, finding joints either too wide or too tight, use pieces of hardboard or plywood, 10–15 mm thick, as spacers. Insert them between the slabs to gauge the distance.

Joints
Continue brushing until the
joints are filled and level

Staggered joints
Make sure that
the segments are
centred with
adjacent joints

Bass broom
Use a stiff
broom to move
the mortar mix
around

5 Make sure, when you come to fitting the radius brick units, that the joints are staggered with the large radius pavers.

6 Finally, shovel the dry-mix mortar (a mixture of 2 parts sand to 1 part lime) over the slabs. Use the bass broom to spread and sweep it evenly into all the joints. Spray water over the whole circle.

Multicoloured crazy paving path

This path draws its inspiration from the hard colours and cool curves of the 1950s.

It is relatively cheap to make, and will inject retro zing into any garden. You can

choose the colour selection according to your personal artistic vision.

TIME

A weekend (about eight hours to prepare the site and fit the kerbstones, and eight hours to lay the slabs).

SAFETY

Slabs sometimes spit out splinters when being broken, so wear goggles if you have to trim any.

YOU WILL NEED

Materials *for a path 4.5 m long and 1 m wide*
- Concrete "York stone" blocks: 20 blocks, 450 mm long, 150 mm wide and 65 mm thick
- Broken concrete paving slabs: about 5 square metres
- Concrete: 1 part (50 kg) cement, 2 parts (100 kg) sharp sand, 3 parts (150 kg) aggregate
- Shingle: 1 tonne medium-sized shingle (pea gravel)
- Sharp sand: 1 tonne
For the dry-mix mortar:
- Lime: 25 kg
- Cement: 25 kg
- Sand: 100 kg (taken from the tonne of sharp sand)

Tools
- Wooden pegs and string line
- Wheelbarrow
- Spade
- Bricklayer's trowel
- Mason's hammer
- Shovel
- Rake
- Spirit level
- Walking board: about 900 mm long, 300 mm wide and 30 mm thick
- Sledgehammer
- Bass broom

COOL, CRAZY COLOURS

The good thing about a crazy paving path is that it can be as wide and curvy as you like, because it doesn't have to conform to the limitations of a particular size of slab. If you have a fancy for a path that snakes around the beds and borders, crazy paving is a good option. Better still, the pieces of broken concrete slab are cheap, so you get a longer path for your money.

Consider how a path might complement the shape of your garden. Visit manufacturers and builder's merchants to look at the available slabs. Some slabs are smooth on one side and heavily textured on the other, with the colour running through the thickness, while others are smooth on both sides and have only one coloured face. When you have made your selection, play around with the broken pieces to see how they might fit together to create an overall uniformity. Plan out the route of the path and mark the edges with pegs and string. Clear the ground down to a depth of 150 mm, making it 1 m wide. Dig a trench at either side of it, 250 mm wide and with a total depth of 250 mm.

CROSS-SECTION ACROSS THE WIDTH OF THE PATH

Block edging
Double-sided "York stone" edging

Crazy paving
Piece of broken paving slab

Dry-mix mortar
Sand, cement and lime brushed into the joints

Soil level
Soil compacted against side of edging

Sand
45 mm deep Raked, smoothed and compacted

Shingle
70 mm deep Raked and levelled

Soil
Raked and compacted

Concrete
A stiff mix pounded into the trench

Trench
250 mm deep A crisp, clean trench

Multicoloured crazy paving path

Tight curves
*Blocks broken to
make a smooth curve*

Dry-mix mortar
*Sand, cement
and lime brushed
into the joints
and damped
down with water*

Edging
*Double-sided "York stone"
blocks, 450 x 150 x 65 mm*

Pavers
*Different colours
distributed evenly*

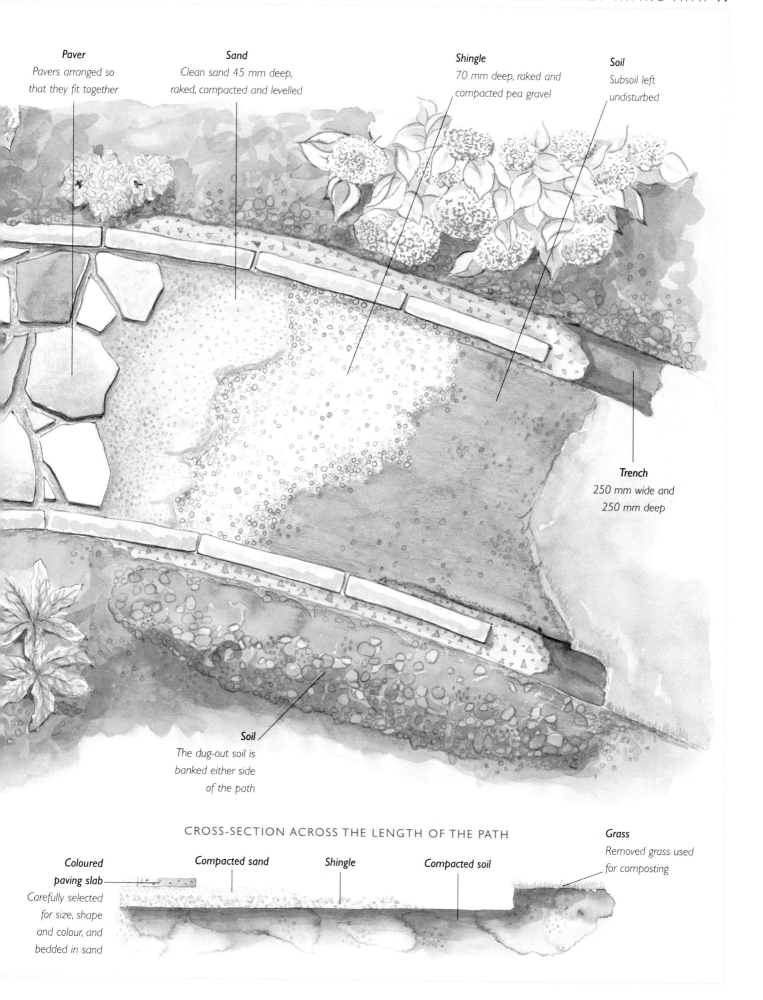

Paver
Pavers arranged so
that they fit together

Sand
Clean sand 45 mm deep,
raked, compacted and levelled

Shingle
70 mm deep, raked and
compacted pea gravel

Soil
Subsoil left
undisturbed

Trench
250 mm wide and
250 mm deep

Soil
The dug-out soil is
banked either side
of the path

CROSS-SECTION ACROSS THE LENGTH OF THE PATH

Grass
Removed grass used
for composting

**Coloured
paving slab**
Carefully selected
for size, shape
and colour, and
bedded in sand

Compacted sand

Shingle

Compacted soil

Step-by-step: **Making the multicoloured crazy paving path**

Concrete
Be generous with the amount of concrete

Raking
Rake the shingle to a depth of 70 mm

Levelling
Use the trowel handle to nudge the blocks into position

Cavity
Push the shingle right into the kerb trench

Compacting
Firm up the shingle with your feet

1 Fill the two trenches with concrete, up to the base level of the path. Carefully set the concrete edging blocks in place to make the kerb. With the bricklayer's trowel and mason's hammer, adjust the blocks so that three-quarters of the block rises above the path base.

2 Shovel the shingle over the earth in the path area and rake it to a depth of 70 mm. Push it into the cavity alongside the edging blocks, and generally rake it so that it follows the level of the ground. Use the spirit level to see whether it is true, and even out by raking if necessary.

Sand level
Keep the sand 35 mm below the kerb stones

3 Cover the shingle with a layer of sand to a depth of about 45 mm. Rake it level and stamp it down so that the surface is about 35 mm lower than the top of the kerb. Check that it is level with the spirit level.

Sand depth
Aim for a depth of 45 mm

Helpful hint

It's always a good idea, when ordering sand and shingle, to specify "well washed". This will minimize the chances of the sand and shingle being contaminated with clay or salt. You cannot use salty sand in concrete or mortar mixes, because it will damage it.

Spacing
Leave a gap of 25 mm
between the pavers

4 Set the pieces of broken slab into place on the sand, leaving about 25 mm between them. Try and position the pieces so that there is a good spread of the various colours.

Laying the slabs
Bed the slabs into the sand

Colours
Aim for an even spread of colours

Walking board
Stand on the board so that you do not dislodge the slabs

Levelling
Use the sledgehammer to help level and embed the slabs

5 Put the walking board on the path and use your weight and the sledgehammer to thump the slabs into place, so that they sit firmly in the sand.

Brushing
Move the dry-mix mortar around with a broom

Dry-mix mortar
Make sure the cement, sand and lime are well blended

6 Make a dry-mix mortar of 4 parts sand, I part cement and I part lime, and sweep it over the path with the bass broom, so that it falls into all the cracks. Spray with water. Leave for 24 hours.

Tranquil Japanese garden

What better way of creating an area of calm, reflection and tranquility, than to build a traditional Japanese garden? It's a beautiful, simple concept that involves gathering a number of basic elements – a traditional lantern, natural rocks and crushed stone – and then carefully arranging them to form a three-dimensional picture.

TIME

Two weekends (about eight hours to build the frame and level the site, sixteen hours to build the lantern, and eight hours to assemble the whole thing).

SAFETY

Building the lantern involves moving a number of back-breaking lumps of stone, so use a sack barrow and get someone to help you.

YOU WILL NEED

Materials *for a garden 2.4 m square*
- Wooden beams: 4 treated posts, 2.4 m long, 100 mm wide and 100 mm thick
- Pegs: 4 pieces of scrap wood, about 25 mm square and 150 mm long
- Woven plastic sheet, 2.4 m square
- Shingle: 500 kg washed shingle
- Boulders: 3 large limestone rocks
- Split sandstone: 4 or 5 large slices of stone
- Mortar: 2 parts (10 kg) cement, 1 part (5 kg) lime, 9 parts (45 kg) soft sand
- Oyster shell grit: 100 kg washed grit
- Lantern base: block of salvaged weathered cut limestone, about 380 mm square and 140 mm thick
- Lantern column: block of salvaged weathered cut limestone, 700 mm long, 300 mm wide and 130 mm thick
- Lantern table: slab of salvaged weathered cut limestone, 300 mm square and 110 mm thick

- Lantern pillars: slab of salvaged weathered cut limestone, 240 mm long, 180 mm wide and 50 mm thick
- Lantern roof: slab of salvaged weathered cut limestone, 300 mm square and 50 mm thick
- Roof finial: slab of salvaged weathered cut limestone, 150 mm square and 50 mm thick
- Finial cobble: a large feature stone, about 100 mm in diameter

Tools
- Tape measure, square and chalk
- Crosscut saw
- Mallet and 25 mm-wide woodworking chisel
- Electric drill fitted with a 25 mm-diameter woodworking drill bit
- Bucket
- Shovel
- Rake
- Fork
- Sack barrow
- Pointing trowel
- Spirit level
- Electric angle grinder with a stone-cutting disc

THE WORLD IN STONE

Think of the items in a Japanese garden as being elements that symbolize our physical and spiritual world – stones are mountains, raked grit is flowing water, large stones are guardians, stone lanterns light our path, and so on. The whole idea is to create a three-dimensional picture of the world. First you build the frame, then "paint" the scene with the stones.

The stone lantern is made from carefully selected pieces of salvaged stone. The four little pillars that support the lantern roof slab are made up of briquettes. These are cut by a simple procedure that involves using an angle grinder to score lines part-way through a limestone slab, first on one side and then on the other, before snapping the slab. The sides of the briquettes reveal a beautiful texture, the result of a machined face and a natural break. The secret of creating a really stunning lantern is to obtain stones with character – visit an architectural salvage company for the best choice, and spend time making your selection.

CROSS-SECTION OF THE JAPANESE GARDEN

Lantern approximately 1.3 m high

Oyster shell Known variously as "turkey grit" or "poultry grit"

Feature stone Chosen for its size, shape and character

Shingle Pea-size, washed and graded

Wooden frame

Plastic sheet

Tranquil Japanese garden

SIDE VIEW OF THE LANTERN

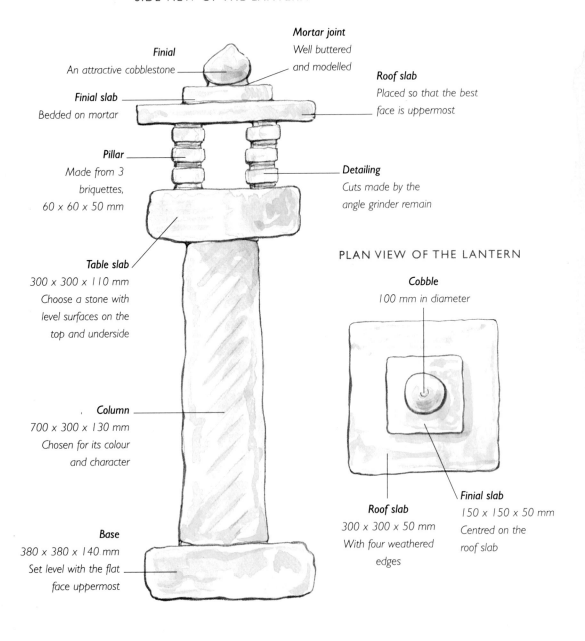

Finial
An attractive cobblestone

Mortar joint
Well buttered
and modelled

Roof slab
Placed so that the best
face is uppermost

Finial slab
Bedded on mortar

Pillar
Made from 3
briquettes,
60 x 60 x 50 mm

Detailing
Cuts made by the
angle grinder remain

Table slab
300 x 300 x 110 mm
Choose a stone with
level surfaces on the
top and underside

Column
700 x 300 x 130 mm
Chosen for its colour
and character

Base
380 x 380 x 140 mm
Set level with the flat
face uppermost

PLAN VIEW OF THE LANTERN

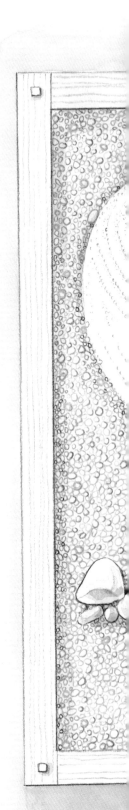

Cobble
100 mm in diameter

Roof slab
300 x 300 x 50 mm
With four weathered
edges

Finial slab
150 x 150 x 50 mm
Centred on the
roof slab

DETAIL OF THE JOINT USED TO MAKE THE WOOD FRAME

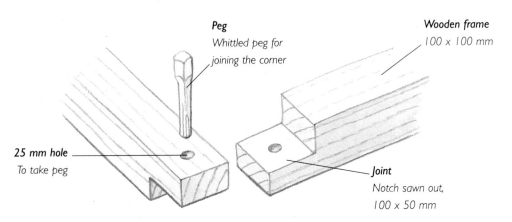

Peg
Whittled peg for
joining the corner

Wooden frame
100 x 100 mm

25 mm hole
To take peg

Joint
Notch sawn out,
100 x 50 mm

PLAN VIEW OF THE GARDEN

Split sandstone
A "mountain" created using layers of stone

Boulders
To support and enhance the layered stone

Shingle
Washed and raked

Lantern
The best viewing angle orientated towards the house

Wooden frame
4 pieces, 2.4 m long, and free from knots and splits near the ends

Feature stone
A large stone positioned half-way between the "river" and the lantern, with a contrasting small stone next to it

Plastic sheet
A woven plastic sheet prevents weeds from growing through the shingle but allows water to drain away

Oyster shell
"River" created by raking the shell

Wooden peg
The peg is left proud for decoration

Step-by-step: Making the tranquil Japanese garden

Shingle
Make sure that the shingle has been washed and is free from salt

Shovel
Use the shovel to spread out the shingle

1 Construct the wooden frame. Draw it out using the tape measure, square and chalk. Remove the waste with the crosscut saw, mallet and chisel. Drill holes as shown in the illustration on page 84. Use the chisel to whittle the pegs out of scrap wood, and put the frame together. Position it in the garden. Cover the ground inside it with the plastic sheet, tucking the edges under the frame. Shovel the shingle over it.

Stone
Use the stones to build a miniature mountain

Fork
A fork is the best tool for raking the shell

River
Leave a channel through the shingle for making the "river" feature

Oyster shell
Obtained as grit from poultry suppliers

Making waves
Drag the fork to make a ridge and furrow pattern

2 Start placing the symbolic features. Rake the shingle into mounds to make areas of "high ground", then carefully position the boulders and sandstone slabs to create "mountains" and "hills".

3 Decide which area of the garden is to be "water", then spread a thick layer of crushed oyster shell over it. Rake the shell with the prongs of the fork to create "ripples" and "waves".

Column
Make sure the lantern column is vertical

Wedging
You may need to use small pieces of stone to wedge the column

4 Position the base block of the lantern. Butter the base of the column stone with mortar, using the pointing trowel. Set the column in place. Check that it is vertical with the spirit level and then leave until the mortar has stiffened. Butter the top of the column with mortar, and lower the lantern table into position.

Helpful hint

The best you can do when testing a rugged piece of stone with a spirit level is to aim for what was traditionally known as "best fit" – meaning you take readings from all sides and make a judgement.

Pillars
Tap the blocks straight

Finial slab
Carefully set the finial slab in place

Mortar
Butter the blocks with the mortar

Mortar
Butter the roof slab with mortar

Roof slab
Make sure the slab is well bedded on to the pillars

5 Set out the dimensions of the briquettes with the tape measure and chalk, and use the angle grinder to cut them out. Butter them with mortar and build the little pillars. Tap down with the trowel handle to adjust the levels.

6 Spread mortar on top of the four pillars. Place the roof slab on the pillars, and butter it with mortar. Carefully position the final slab. Set the feature cobble in place, fixing it with mortar that is modelled to fit the contours of the stone.

Dry-stone retaining wall

Crisscrossing hill and dale, dry-stone walls are the traditional way of controlling livestock and marking boundaries. The technique evolved over many thousands of years. It does not require cement or mortar – just stone upon stone to create a beautiful structure that is uniquely capable of withstanding the weather.

YOU WILL NEED

Materials *for a wall*
4.8 m long and 800 mm high
- Split stone (sandstone or limestone): 1.5 tonnes
- Hardcore for the foundation (either waste stone or builder's rubble): 5 wheelbarrow loads
- Keystone: attractive heavy stone, about 300 mm long, 200 mm wide, 200 mm thick

Tools
- Wheelbarrow
- Spade and shovel
- Tape measure
- String line
- Club hammer
- Bolster chisel
- Piece of old carpet
- Bricklayer's trowel
- Spirit level
- Rake

A PERFECT PATTERN OF STONE

This wall stands about 800 mm high for three-quarters of its length, then runs in a gentle curve down to meet the ground. Study your site and work out the total length of the wall that you intend to build. Reckon on ordering about 1 tonne of stone for every 3-metre length of wall (you will also need about 3 wheelbarrow loads of hardcore). It's a good idea to add on about ten per cent extra for good measure. When you visit the stoneyard, select split stone about 30–100 mm thick, with a flat top and bottom, and a reasonably straight face edge. Choose a firm stone, rather than a stone that crumbles and flakes to the touch. Select rougher, character stones for the coping, such as pieces of weathered stone (maybe even large lumps, rather than slices). Don't forget that you will need hardcore for the foundation trench – this project uses waste stone, but you could also use broken brick, a mixture of gravel and clay, pulverized concrete or whatever else is available.

CROSS-SECTION DETAIL
OF THE DRY-STONE WALL

Coping
A line of stones, on edge, to finish the wall

Stone
Split sandstone, limestone or broken pavers

Plants
Plants to reinforce the coping

Earth
The earth is retained by the wall

Tie stones
The occasional use of long stones provides extra stability, tying the wall to the earth

Stone chips
Small pieces of stone used to maintain level

Earth
Firmed up against the base of the wall

Foundation
Compacted rubble

Dry-stone retaining wall

PLAN VIEW OF THE WALL

Keystone
A large stone to hold back the coping stones

Large tie stone
Runs back into the retained soil to provide stability and support

Gaps for plants
Hardy plants pushed into the gaps

Coping stones
Coping stones are set on steps so that the string of stones runs down in a smooth slope

Split stone
Stones angled to show the curve to best advantage

Compacted soil
Soil hammered between the coping stones

Stepped courses
Step the courses to create flat surfaces for the coping stones

Keystone
300 x 200 x 200 mm Well-bedded, heavy stone to act as a buttress

Compacted soil
Soil pounded into the cavities

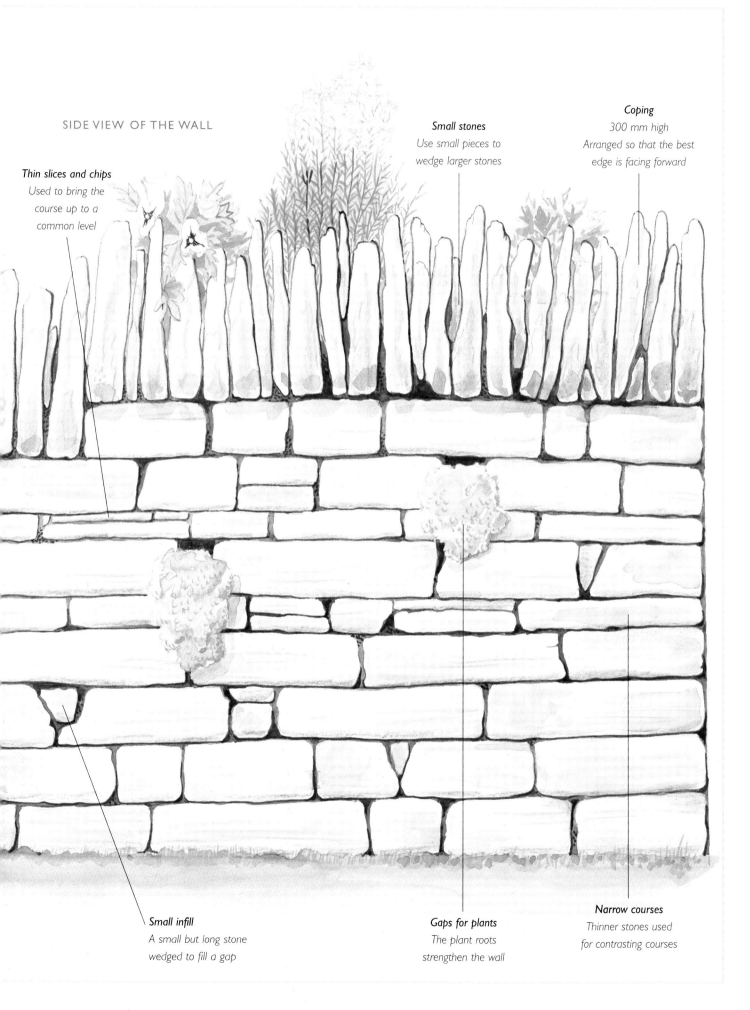

SIDE VIEW OF THE WALL

Small stones
Use small pieces to
wedge larger stones

Coping
300 mm high
Arranged so that the best
edge is facing forward

Thin slices and chips
Used to bring the
course up to a
common level

Small infill
A small but long stone
wedged to fill a gap

Gaps for plants
The plant roots
strengthen the wall

Narrow courses
Thinner stones used
for contrasting courses

Step-by-step: **Making the dry-stone retaining wall**

Earth bank
Slope the bank so it does
not fall into the trench

Club hammer
Use a medium-weight
club hammer

Hardcore
Pound the
hardcore with
the club
hammer to
make a solid
foundation.
Level it off
with earth

Protection
Wear strong
gloves to
protect your
hands

Carpet
Place carpet
underneath
the stone

1 Dig away the earth to reveal the bank of earth that needs retaining. Mark out a trench about 300 mm wide and 200 mm deep with the string line and tape measure, then excavate it and fill it with compacted hardcore. Level it with earth.

2 Use the club hammer and the bolster chisel to cut your stock of stone into reasonably-sized pieces. Support the stone on the carpet, set the chisel squarely on top, and then strike the chisel with a single, well-placed blow.

Tamping
Use the wooden handle
to align the stones

3 Lay the first row of stones on the levelled foundation, and use the bricklayer's trowel to rake earth down from the bank to support the row. Lay another row, rake down some more earth, and so on. Use the club hammer to compact the supporting earth and to tamp individual stones into place. Leave hand-sized spaces now and again to form planting pockets.

Bank of earth
Rake the
earth down to
the level of
each stone

Coursing
Adjust the stones so that they are all level

4 At staggered intervals along the rows – say about every metre – carefully select long "tie" stones, and place them so that they run back into the bank. Beat the earth into place around the stones. Check that everything is level with the spirit level.

"Tie" stone
Run the stone into the bank and secure it with earth

Helpful hint

Select the long "tie" stones with care. Go for stones that are slightly broader and thicker at the back end – so that most of the weight is anchored into the bank. This helps to give the wall greater stability.

Wedging
Use small stones to wedge the coping stones

Slivers
Insert slivers of stone to adjust the coursing level

Coping stones
Select character stones for the coping course

Cavities
Gaps between the stones can be filled with turf

Sighting
Look down the wall to spot stones that require tapping into line

5 When you have a good wall, wet the surrounding earth and rake it over the top course. Press a row of vertical coping stones into the mud to top off the wall. Rake earth up and between the coping stones, and pound into place.

6 Sight down the finished wall, bang earth into cavities, and tap misfit stones back into line. Adjust individual stones by banging small slivers of waste stone into the cavities.

Inspirations: Dry stone

While wood and wire fences can be intimidating and visually intrusive, and hedges need a lot of upkeep, dry-stone walls melt into the landscape and require the minimum of maintenance. A well-built dry-stone wall can, at one and the same time, protect, exclude, retain, suggest stability, or simply guide the eye from one part of the garden to another. A dry-stone wall or sculpture speaks of permanence.

ABOVE Slate setts used in a new path. The technique of setting slate on edge is common in Cornwall, England, and seen in cottages, quays and churches.

ABOVE A traditional old dry-stone wall in North Devon, England, made from local fieldstone. Ivy-leaved toadflax has colonized the nooks and crannies. The wall is superbly crafted, and the colour and texture of the stone harmonize perfectly with the location.

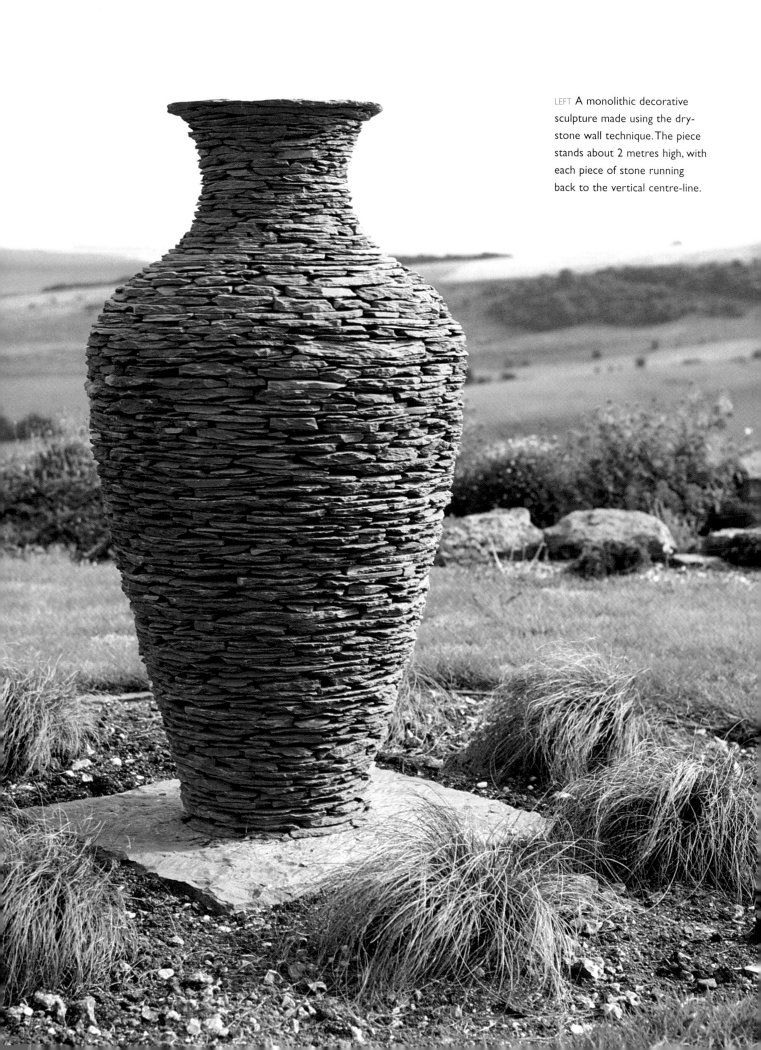

A monolithic decorative
sculpture made using the dry-
stone wall technique. The piece
stands about 2 metres high, with
each piece of stone running
back to the vertical centre-line.

Cantilevered seat-shelf

If you would like to build something that uses a massive stone slab and not much else, and you have a good solid wall in your garden, then a cantilevered seat-shelf is a really great idea. The seat looks like it is floating on air!

TIME

A weekend to build (eight hours for fixing the iron support bars, and eight hours for shaping the copper sleeves and placing the stone).

SAFETY

Working with the resin capsules is potentially dangerous, so follow the manufacturer's directions very carefully.

YOU WILL NEED

Materials *for a seat-shelf 1.3 m (or up to 2 m) long and 400 mm wide*
• Sill stone: a single salvaged sill stone, 1.3 m to 2 m long, 400 mm wide and 50 mm thick
• Iron reinforcing bar: 2 m long and 20 mm in diameter
• Anchor resin capsules: 3 epoxy acrylate resin capsules, 20 mm in diameter, suitable for fixing metal to stone
• Copper pipe (as used by plumbers): 3 x 550 mm long, 25 mm in diameter

Tools
• Tape measure and piece of chalk
• Large-size angle grinder with cutting discs for metal and stone
• Electric jack-hammer drill fitted with a 25 mm masonry bit (long enough to drill a hole 200 mm deep)
• Mason's hammer
• Spirit level
• A short length of railway sleeper
• Claw hammer

FLOATING ON AIR

Though this might appear to be a very simple project – no more than a stone slab suspended on cantilevered bars – a lot of work goes into its creation. But if the idea of working with a giant-size drill and a massive angle grinder appeals to you, you will find it fun. The seat-shelf must be sited against a wall at least 250 mm thick, made from solid brick, concrete block, or stone (either the wall of your house, or, better still, a freestanding wall in the garden). The iron reinforcing rods are glued into place by means of anchor resin capsules (sealed glass tubes filled with epoxy resin, a hardener, and granules of stone). The glass tube is eased down the drilled hole, and the iron bar is hammered and twisted into place – the glass breaks, the chemicals mix and cure, and the bar is glued into place. The finished seat-shelf will hold three people, or their equivalent weight in plant pots!

PLAN VIEW OF THE SEAT-SHELF

Wall

Sill stone
Selected for its colour and texture

Anchor resin
A resin capsule is used to fix the bar

Copper pipe
Rolled ends for decorative effect

Iron reinforcing bar
Set 350 mm from the ground

Brick patio

Hardcore

Wall foundation

Cantilevered seat-shelf

FRONT VIEW AND PLAN VIEW OF SEAT SHELF

Fixing
The weight of the sill stone holds it in place

Sill stone
1.3 to 2 m x 400 x 50 mm
Arranged so that the weathered (textured) edge faces forwards

Copper pipe
Rolled end projects from under the sill

Sill stone
The textured side faces upwards

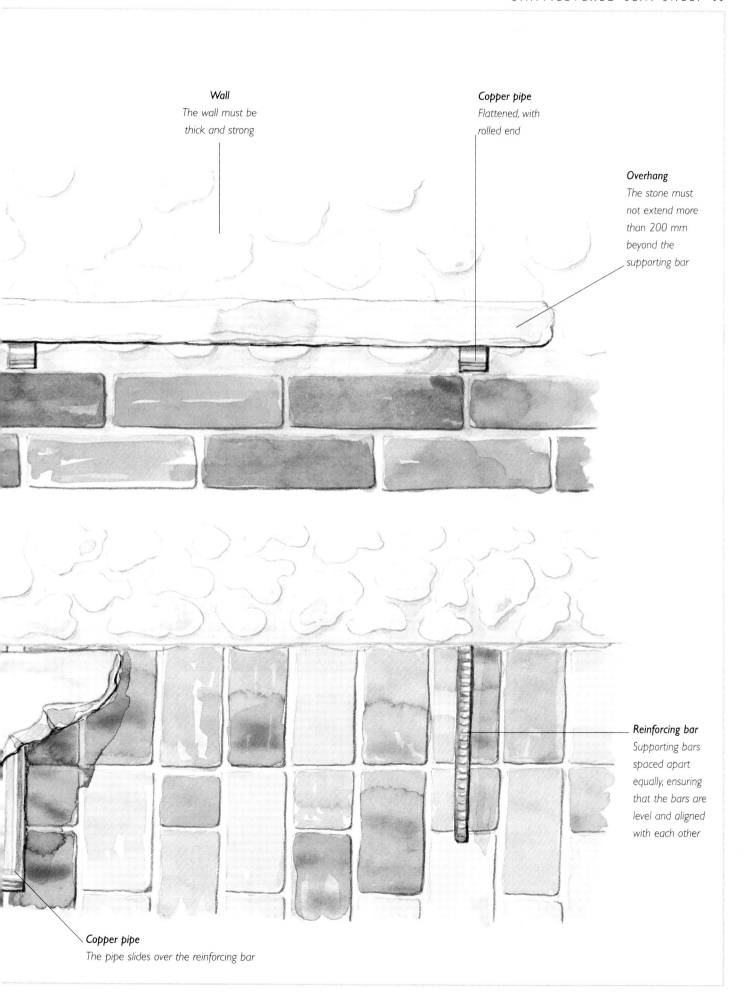

Wall
The wall must be
thick and strong

Copper pipe
Flattened, with
rolled end

Overhang
The stone must
not extend more
than 200 mm
beyond the
supporting bar

Reinforcing bar
Supporting bars
spaced apart
equally, ensuring
that the bars are
level and aligned
with each other

Copper pipe
The pipe slides over the reinforcing bar

Step-by-step: Making the cantilevered seat-shelf

Grinder shield
Always have the shield in place

Protection
Wear gloves, goggles and a dust-mask

Grinder angle
Keep the disc at right angles to the stone

Metal cutting
Use a disc designed for cutting metal

Iron bar
Stand on the bar so that it stays still

1 Mark out the sill stone to size. Fit the angle grinder with the stone-cutting disc and trim the back edge of the stone slab to a square finish, so that it measures precisely 400 mm wide. Leave the weathered front and side edges intact.

2 Change the disc to the one for cutting metal and cut the iron bar into four lengths – three at 550 mm and one at 350 mm. Make sure your feet are well away from the line of cut.

Hole position
Avoid drilling very hard stones such as granite

3 With the drill, run three holes, 200 mm deep, into the wall. These should be level, 350 mm up from the ground and about 500 mm apart.

Level
All three holes must be level with each other

Drill
Large, powerful drills can be hired from a specialist shop

MAKING THE CANTILEVERED SEAT-SHELF **101**

Loading the hole
Clear out any dust and push the
capsule to the end of the hole

Resin capsules
Handle the
capsules with
great care

4 Slide an anchor capsule
into a hole, follow it up
with one of the long iron bars,
and then hammer the bar with
the mason's hammer to break the
glass of the capsule. Make sure
that the bar is in the correct
position and square to the wall,
using the spirit level, then leave it
until the resin has set.

Helpful hint

Even though you are
wearing goggles, make sure,
when you come to breaking
the glass capsule, that you
stand well to one side – so
that you are out of the
firing line if the resin squirts
out of the hole.

Copper pipe
Bang the flattened pipe
end around the iron bar

Level
Make sure the three bars
are level with each other

Railway sleeper
Use the
sleeper to hold
the iron bar

Bar
The bar must
be set at
right angles to
the wall

Copper
The cut end of
the pipe should
touch the wall

5 Drill a 25 mm hole into the railway
sleeper and bang the short length of
iron bar into place. One piece at a time,
take a length of copper pipe, flatten 150 mm
at the end with the claw hammer, and bend
the flat section around the iron bar.

6 Finally, slide the copper sleeves over
the iron bars, check with the spirit
level to ensure all is level, and lift the slab
into position. Its weight holds it in place.

Sundial

The classic garden sundial must surely be one of the most useful and interesting items to have in the garden. What better way of passing a hot and lazy summer's day than to lounge in the garden and watch as the sundial's shadowy finger slowly but surely marks off the hours? This design fits on an existing patio or other surface.

YOU WILL NEED

Materials *for a sundial 640 mm high and 400 mm square*
- Mortar: 2 parts (20 kg) cement, 1 part (10 kg) lime, 9 parts (90 kg) soft sand
- Flagstone for the base: a salvaged stone about 400 mm square and 80 mm thick
- Flagstone for the table: a salvaged stone about 300 mm square and 60 mm thick
- Split slate: 50 kg of broken pieces
- Split sandstone: 50 kg of broken pieces
- A brass sundial of your choice
- Screws and plugs to fit the holes in the brass plate

Tools
- Wheelbarrow
- Bucket
- Tape measure and piece of chalk
- Pointing trowel
- Spirit level
- Mason's hammer
- Drill fitted with a masonry bit (size to match holes in sundial plate)
- Screwdriver to fit the screws

A SUNNY WAY TO PASS THE TIME

When deciding where to put the sundial, you not only have to consider how the structure relates to the design of the garden, but the position must also be one that gets sufficient sunshine in order for the sundial to work. If your garden is mostly surrounded by tall trees, settle for a position that gets the best of the sunshine when you are most likely to be resting in the garden – maybe after lunch, or late in the afternoon.

The structure is made up of four elements – a flagstone slab for the base, a plinth built up from pieces of sandstone, a cylindrical column constructed from pieces of slate, and another flagstone slab for the table. Mortar holds the whole thing together. In order to successfully align the square brass dial with the square slabs that go to make the base and the table, it is necessary, right from start, to orientate the brass slab towards the sun, so that the dial is showing the correct time. Building can then proceed.

CROSS-SECTION OF THE SUNDIAL

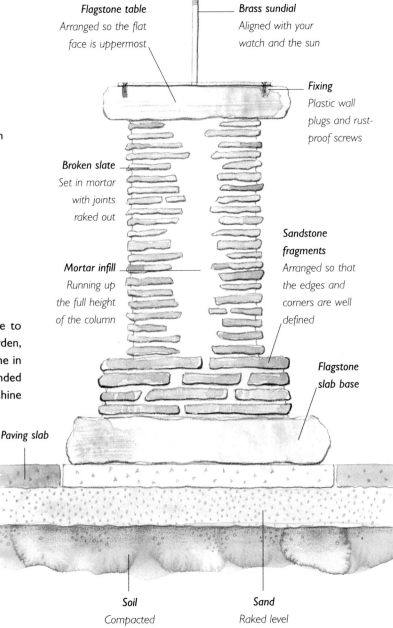

Flagstone table *Arranged so the flat face is uppermost*

Brass sundial *Aligned with your watch and the sun*

Fixing *Plastic wall plugs and rust-proof screws*

Broken slate *Set in mortar with joints raked out*

Sandstone fragments *Arranged so that the edges and corners are well defined*

Mortar infill *Running up the full height of the column*

Flagstone slab base

Paving slab

Soil *Compacted*

Sand *Raked level*

Sundial

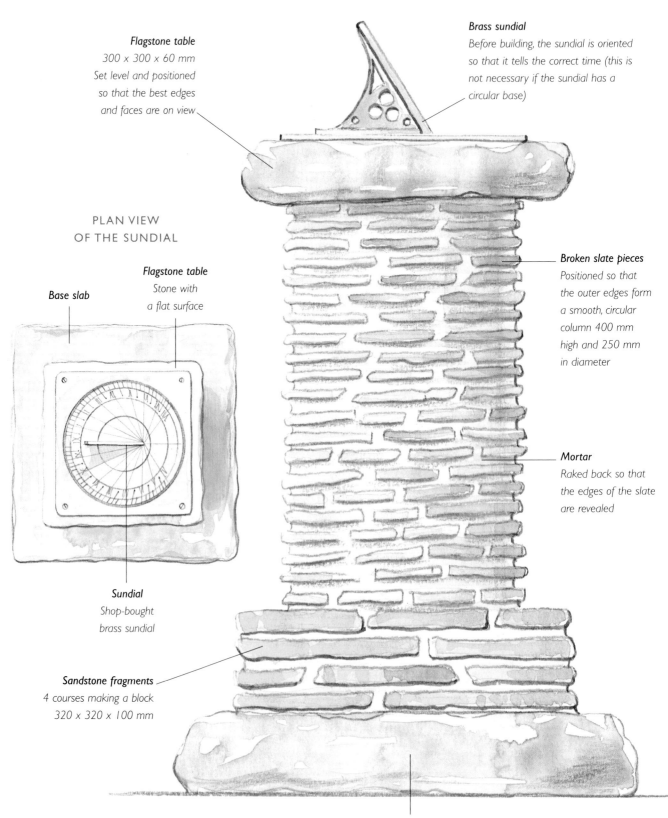

SIDE VIEW OF THE SUNDIAL

Flagstone table
300 x 300 x 60 mm
Set level and positioned
so that the best edges
and faces are on view

Brass sundial
Before building, the sundial is oriented
so that it tells the correct time (this is
not necessary if the sundial has a
circular base)

PLAN VIEW
OF THE SUNDIAL

Flagstone table
Stone with
a flat surface

Base slab

Broken slate pieces
Positioned so that
the outer edges form
a smooth, circular
column 400 mm
high and 250 mm
in diameter

Mortar
Raked back so that
the edges of the slate
are revealed

Sundial
Shop-bought
brass sundial

Sandstone fragments
4 courses making a block
320 x 320 x 100 mm

Flagstone base slab
400 x 400 x 80 mm

EXPLODED VIEW OF THE SUNDIAL

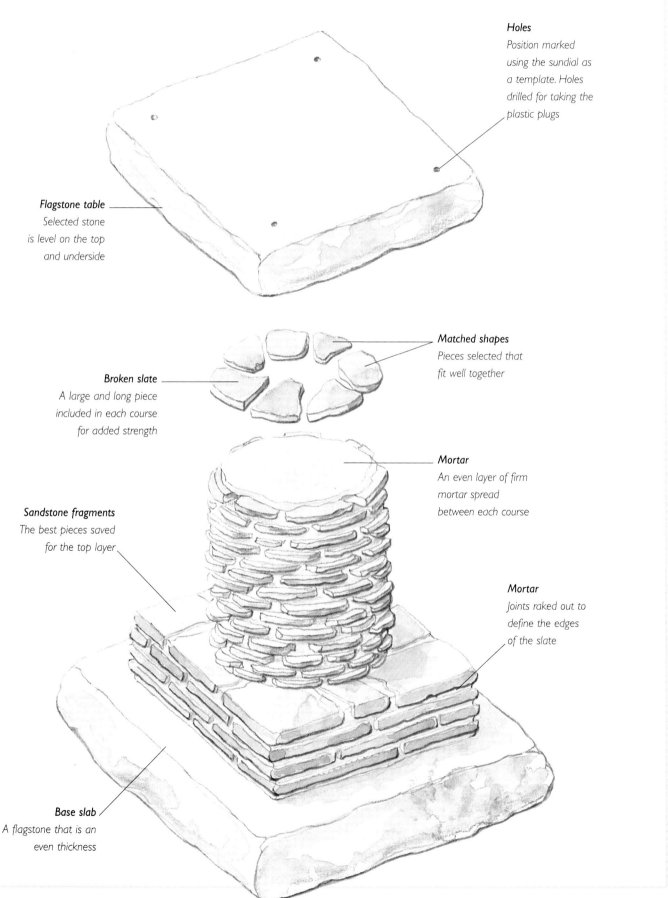

Holes
*Position marked
using the sundial as
a template. Holes
drilled for taking the
plastic plugs*

Flagstone table
*Selected stone
is level on the top
and underside*

Matched shapes
*Pieces selected that
fit well together*

Broken slate
*A large and long piece
included in each course
for added strength*

Mortar
*An even layer of firm
mortar spread
between each course*

Sandstone fragments
*The best pieces saved
for the top layer*

Mortar
*Joints raked out to
define the edges
of the slate*

Base slab
*A flagstone that is an
even thickness*

Step-by-step: **Making the sundial**

Alignment
Rotate the base to match the
orientation of the sundial

I Put the brass sundial plate on the ground, check the orientation against the sun and your watch, then set the stone base slab on mortar, aligning it with the brass plate.

Levelling
Use slivers of
stone to adjust
the level if
necessary

Bedding
Bed the
slab into
the mortar

Trowel work
Tap the stone with the trowel
handle until it sits correctly

Mortar
Lay a bed of mortar

Slate circle
Arrange the
slate to make
a circle
250 mm in
diameter

Bedding
Press the
slate into the
bed of mortar

Plinth
Build the layers
up to a height
of 100 mm

2 To build the plinth, use the pointing trowel to butter the base with mortar, and arrange the sandstone to make a 320 mm square. Continue until the plinth is about 100 mm high.

3 To build the column, butter mortar on the plinth, and arrange the slate to make a circle 250 mm in diameter. Butter the circle with mortar, add another layer of slate, and so on. Check each layer with the tape measure and spirit level.

Circle circumference
Always aim for a good fit
around the outside edge

4 Continue laying circles of slate until the column is about 400 mm high. If the structure looks as though it is going to sag, tap stones into place with the mason's hammer, and stop to allow the mortar to stiffen up before continuing.

Adjusting
Use the mason's
hammer to tap
proud stones
back into line

Helpful hint

If the day is hot and dry, dip the slate in water prior to bedding it in mortar. This reduces the absorbency of the stone and prevents it drawing all the water out of the mortar. Dip a stone in water, give it a shake and then press it in the mortar.

Screwing
Work carefully to avoid slipping
and damaging the brass

Alignment
Double-check the
orientation of the sundial

Drilling
Use a masonry
bit to bore holes
in the stone

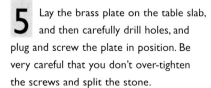

Bedding
Lower the slab
on to the bed
of mortar

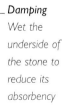

Damping
Wet the
underside of
the stone to
reduce its
absorbency

5 Lay the brass plate on the table slab, and then carefully drill holes, and plug and screw the plate in position. Be very careful that you don't over-tighten the screws and split the stone.

6 Finally, butter the top of the column with mortar and stand the slab and sundial in place. Check the alignment against the sun and your watch.

Flagstone potting table

If you enjoy potting up plants, but are fed up with working on that wobbly bench in the greenhouse, or you simply want to build a beautiful potting table in the nineteenth-century English tradition, this project will prove very satisfactory. The table is perfect for displaying plants when not in use for potting.

TIME

Three days (eight hours to lay the foundation slab, fourteen hours to build the two base piers, and a couple of hours to fit the flagstone).

SAFETY

The flagstone slab is extremely heavy – it needs two strong people to lift it into position.

YOU WILL NEED

Materials *for a table 1 m long, 580 mm wide and 800 mm high*
- Mortar: 2 parts (30 kg) cement, 1 part (15 kg) lime, 9 parts (135 kg) soft sand
- Concrete: 1 part (50 kg) cement, 2 parts (100 kg) sharp sand, 3 parts (150 kg) aggregate
- Slate or limestone flagstone: 1 flagstone about 1 m long, 580 mm wide and 80–90 mm thick
- Split limestone: 1 square metre salvaged roof stone, about 15 mm thick

- Architectural limestone: 8 salvaged cut and faced stones about 250 mm long, 170 mm wide and 130 mm thick

Tools
- Tape measure, straight-edge, piece of chalk
- Spade and shovel
- Wheelbarrow and bucket
- Wooden beam: about 600 mm long, 80 mm wide, and 50 mm thick
- Mortar float
- Bricklayer's trowel
- Mason's hammer
- Pointing trowel
- Spirit level
- Club hammer

A TABLE FOR ALL SEASONS

This table needs to be built against a strong brick or stone wall in the garden. It could also be sited against a shed. Ideally, you need an area that is tucked away and oriented so that the wall shields you from the wind, while the sun warms your back.

The decorative effect of the piers is achieved by building alternate courses of cut architectural limestone and layered roof stone. The mortar has been raked out in order to create strong shadow lines that draw the eye to the stone. When you are searching out your materials, opt for salvaged stone – choose large blocks showing a dressed face to all sides, and roof stone with cut edges. Spend time in the stoneyard stacking and arranging the various materials on offer, until you come up with a suitable combination. While all the given measurements are more or less flexible, if you want to vary them, the only proviso is that the pier walls need to be at least 170 mm thick. If, at any point during construction, the walls begin to sag or the mortar oozes from the joints, stop work until the mortar has stiffened up.

CROSS-SECTION OF THE POTTING TABLE

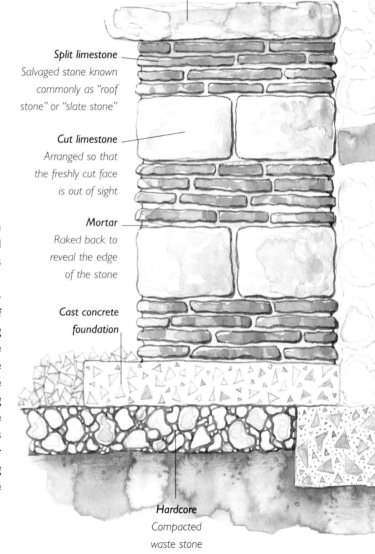

Flagstone table
At least 80 mm thick and set with the weathered surface facing uppermost

Split limestone
Salvaged stone known commonly as "roof stone" or "slate stone"

Cut limestone
Arranged so that the freshly cut face is out of sight

Mortar
Raked back to reveal the edge of the stone

Cast concrete foundation

Hardcore
Compacted waste stone

Flagstone potting table

FRONT VIEW OF THE POTTING TABLE

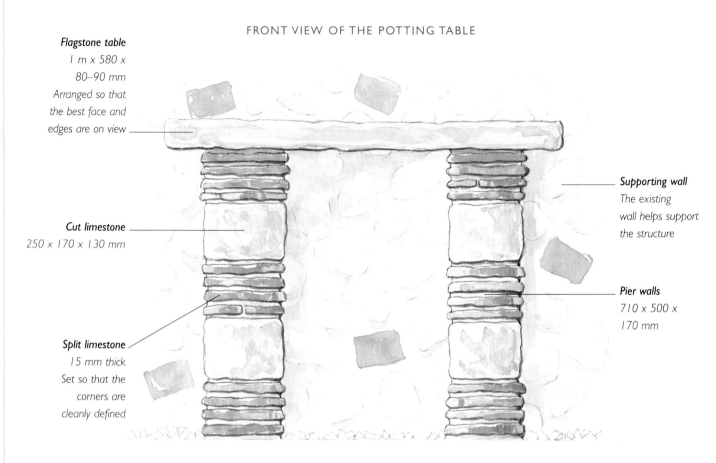

Flagstone table
1 m x 580 x
80–90 mm
Arranged so that
the best face and
edges are on view

Cut limestone
250 x 170 x 130 mm

Split limestone
15 mm thick
Set so that the
corners are
cleanly defined

Supporting wall
The existing
wall helps support
the structure

Pier walls
710 x 500 x
170 mm

PLAN VIEW OF THE POTTING TABLE

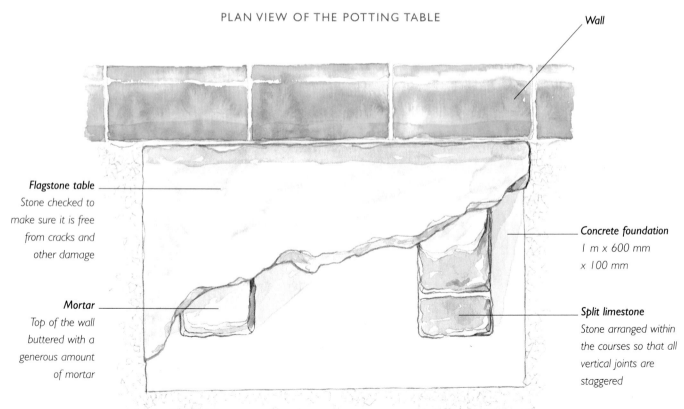

Wall

Flagstone table
Stone checked to
make sure it is free
from cracks and
other damage

Mortar
Top of the wall
buttered with a
generous amount
of mortar

Concrete foundation
1 m x 600 mm
x 100 mm

Split limestone
Stone arranged within
the courses so that all
vertical joints are
staggered

CUT-AWAY VIEW OF THE POTTING TABLE

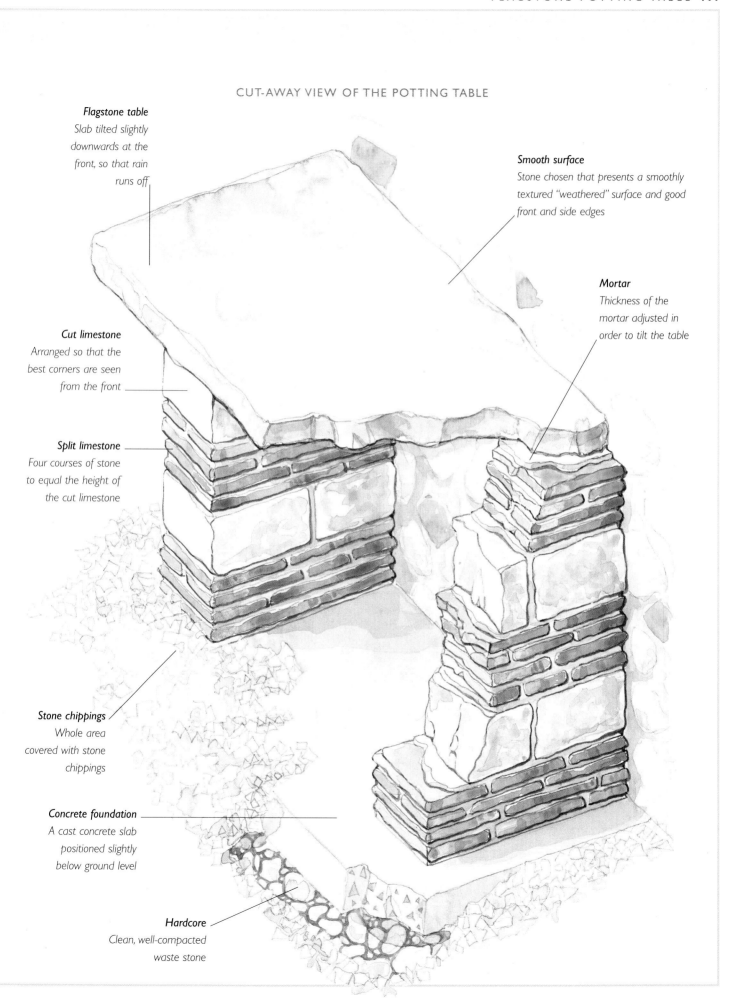

Flagstone table
Slab tilted slightly downwards at the front, so that rain runs off

Smooth surface
Stone chosen that presents a smoothly textured "weathered" surface and good front and side edges

Mortar
Thickness of the mortar adjusted in order to tilt the table

Cut limestone
Arranged so that the best corners are seen from the front

Split limestone
Four courses of stone to equal the height of the cut limestone

Stone chippings
Whole area covered with stone chippings

Concrete foundation
A cast concrete slab positioned slightly below ground level

Hardcore
Clean, well-compacted waste stone

Step-by-step: **Making the flagstone potting table**

Concrete foundation
*Aim for a thickness
of 100 mm*

Piers
*Each pier measures 170 mm
thick and 500 mm wide*

Float
*Use the float
to bring the
concrete to a
smooth finish*

Guidelines
*Use chalk to
mark the
positions of
the piers*

Spacing
*Set the piers
400 mm apart
at the centres*

1 Use the spade to clear the foundation area. Make it 1 m wide, 600 mm from front to back, and 200 mm deep. Half-fill it with hardcore, then top it off with a layer of concrete 100 mm thick. Use the wooden beam and mortar float to bring it to a smooth, level finish.

2 Use the tape measure, chalk and straight-edge to draw out the two piers. They should be 215 mm in from each side of the foundation, and 230 mm apart. They measure 170 mm thick, and 500 mm deep from front to back.

Wall
*The piers must be built
against a wall*

3 Butter mortar on the base slab (within the pier markings) with the bricklayer's trowel, and arrange the first course of split limestone. (Trim it to size with the mason's hammer.) Butter the limestone with mortar, and add another layer. Make sure the corners are as crisp as possible. Insert courses of architectural limestone where appropriate, placing the blocks lengthways to run from front to back of the pier. Continue until the courses reach a total height of 710 mm.

Tapping
*Tap the
limestone with
the handle of
the trowel to
bed it in the
mortar*

Pier height
The piers are
710 mm high

Height
adjustment
The thin layers
of stone allow
for small
adjustments
in height

Architectural
limestone

4 Use the pointing trowel to rake out some of the mortar from between the various courses. Do it after about every three to four courses.

Pointing
Use the point
of the trowel to
clean out the
courses

Helpful hint

When working on a small project like this, use the large bricklayer's trowel to carry and catch the mortar, and the smaller pointing trowel to do the pointing.

Checking levels
Use the club
hammer to tap
the slab into
the mortar

5 When you have built both piers, wait until the mortar has begun to set. Then butter the top of the piers with mortar and bed the table slab in place. Check that it is horizontal with the spirit level. If it is not, tap the offending side of the slab with the hammer.

Finishing
Cover the foundation
slab with your
chosen material

Camomile bench

This simple idea is beautifully effective. The stone bench – a bit like a sofa – has the seat planted out with a mixture of grass and camomile. When you sit down on the camomile, its fragrant scent wafts over you. Buy the non-flowering variety of camomile, *Chamaemelum* 'Treneague', which is used to create camomile lawns.

CROSS-SECTION OF THE BENCH

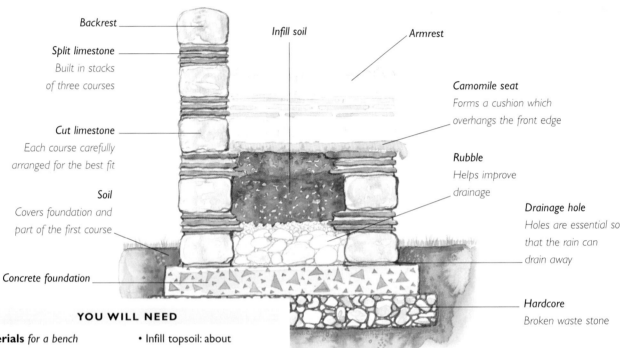

Backrest

Split limestone
Built in stacks of three courses

Cut limestone
Each course carefully arranged for the best fit

Soil
Covers foundation and part of the first course

Concrete foundation

Infill soil

Armrest

Camomile seat
Forms a cushion which overhangs the front edge

Rubble
Helps improve drainage

Drainage hole
Holes are essential so that the rain can drain away

Hardcore
Broken waste stone

YOU WILL NEED

Materials *for a bench 1.57 m long, 730 mm wide and 870 mm high*
- Mortar: 2 parts (70 kg) cement, 1 part (35 kg) lime, 9 parts (315 kg) soft sand
- Concrete: 1 part (150 kg) cement, 2 parts (300 kg) sharp sand, 3 parts (450 kg) aggregate
- Split limestone: 2 square metres of salvaged roof stone, about 15 mm thick
- Architectural limestone: about 60 salvaged cut and faced stones, 250 mm long, 150 mm wide, 90–100 mm thick
- Hardcore: 1 cubic metre

- Infill topsoil: about 3 wheelbarrow loads

Tools
- Wheelbarrow and bucket
- Tape measure, straight-edge, piece of chalk
- Spade and shovel
- Casting beams: 2 beams about 1.6 m long, 80 mm wide and 50 mm thick
- Wooden tamping beam: 1.2 m long, 80 mm wide and 50 mm thick
- Bricklayer's trowel
- Pointing trowel
- Mason's hammer
- Spirit level
- Wire brush

A COMFORTABLE FRAGRANCE

If you have ever walked barefoot over a camomile lawn and marvelled at its fragrance and the feel of the soft, lush growth, you can imagine that sitting on a cushion of camomile will also be a very pleasant experience. Everything about this project is a joy – the bench makes a very comfortable and exotic seat, the structure is large and decorative enough for even the grandest garden, and the notion of sitting on the camomile is so novel that the bench becomes a great conversation piece. The structure is made up from courses of cut architectural stone alternating with courses of stacked roof stone. The mix of stone gives an interesting finish; the courses of roof stone are also used to level out the inevitable mismatch and stepping that occurs when using salvaged architectural stone. The overall pattern of the coursing is further enhanced by the raked mortar joints.

Camomile bench

FRONT VIEW OF THE BENCH

Backrest
Stones arranged so that the back is free from points and dips

Mortar
Pointed on the top course

Cut limestone
250 x 150 x 90–100 mm
Rounded stones chosen for the ends of the armrests

Split limestone
15 mm thick
The best stones selected for the front of the arms

Camomile seat
Seat covered with turf planted with plugs of chamomile

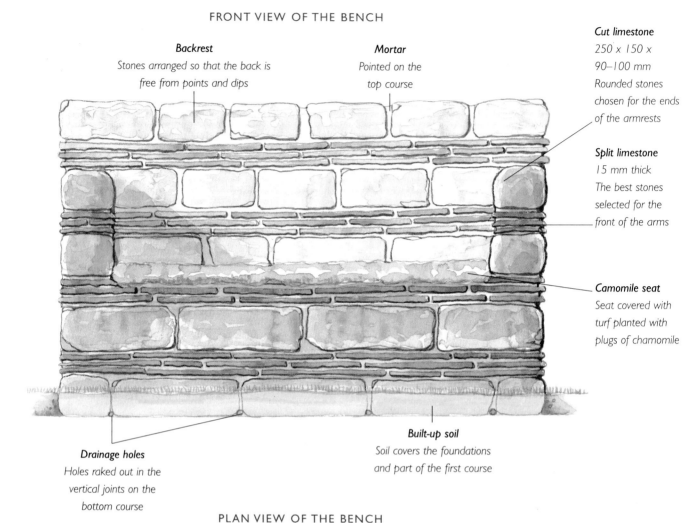

Drainage holes
Holes raked out in the vertical joints on the bottom course

Built-up soil
Soil covers the foundations and part of the first course

PLAN VIEW OF THE BENCH

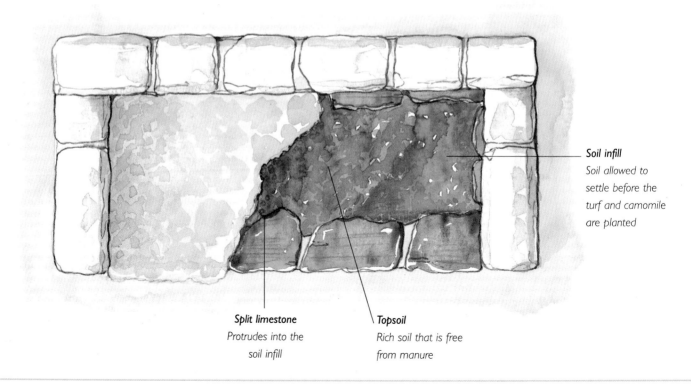

Soil infill
Soil allowed to settle before the turf and camomile are planted

Split limestone
Protrudes into the soil infill

Topsoil
Rich soil that is free from manure

CUT-AWAY VIEW OF THE BENCH

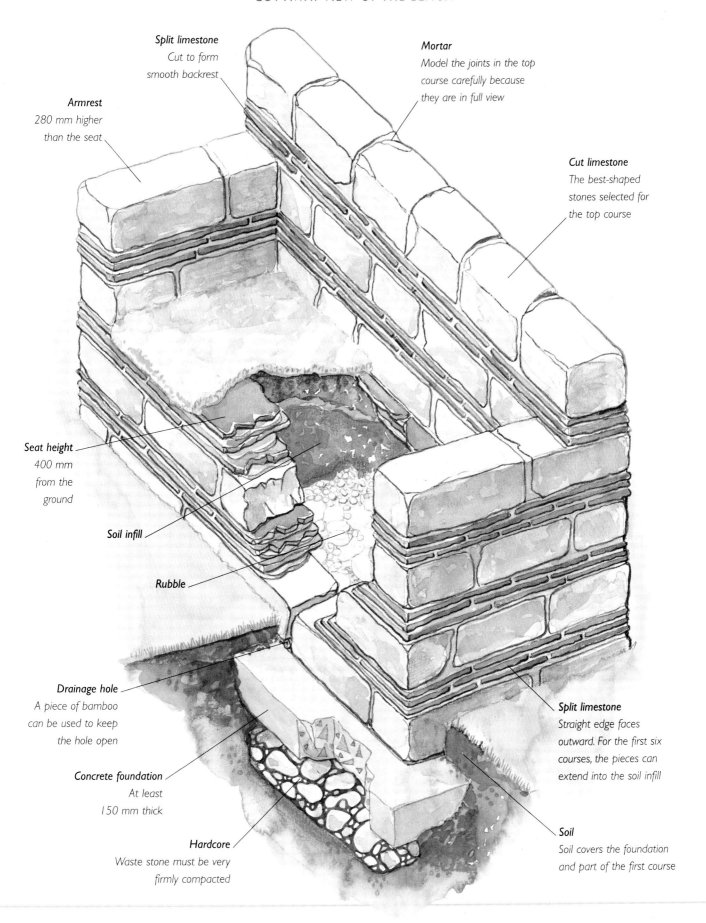

Split limestone
Cut to form
smooth backrest

Mortar
Model the joints in the top
course carefully because
they are in full view

Armrest
280 mm higher
than the seat

Cut limestone
The best-shaped
stones selected for
the top course

Seat height
400 mm
from the
ground

Soil infill

Rubble

Split limestone
Straight edge faces
outward. For the first six
courses, the pieces can
extend into the soil infill

Drainage hole
A piece of bamboo
can be used to keep
the hole open

Concrete foundation
At least
150 mm thick

Hardcore
Waste stone must be very
firmly compacted

Soil
Soil covers the foundation
and part of the first course

Step-by-step: Making the camomile bench

Measuring
Use the tape measure to
set out the outline

Trial fitting
Have a dry fitting
of the stones

Foundation
Make the
concrete slab
150 mm thick

Best face
Arrange the
stones so that
the best face
is on view

Best fit
Swap the
stones around
until you have
a well-fitting
arrangement

1 Excavate to a depth of 300 mm and
half-fill with compacted hardcore.
Position and level the casting beams, 1 m
apart, and top them up with concrete.
Level with the tamping beam. Use the tape
measure, chalk and straight-edge to outline
the bench (1.57 m x 730 mm).

2 Arrange the blocks of salvaged
architectural stone so that they fit
well and the best cut face is looking to the
chalk line. Wet the blocks and use the
bricklayer's trowel and the pointing trowel
to bed them on stiff mortar.

Infill
Pack the bench with top soil

3 To lay the roof stone,
spread a bed of mortar,
and use the mason's hammer to
carefully trim and arrange the
pieces of stone. Repeat until you
have three courses of roof stone.
Lay a layer of architectural stone.
Continue laying the alternating
courses, and keep checking that it
is all level with the spirit level.

Levelling
Check each
course using a
spirit level

Helpful hint

Spend a lot of time
choosing the roof stone
cornerstones and making
sure they are a good fit, and
the rest of the course will
fall into line more easily.

Cornerstone
Position the architectural
cornerstones accurately

Armrest
The armrest
course should
be tied in with
the backrest

Armrest height
Build up to a
height of
280 mm above
the seat level

Backrest
Build the back
using three
courses of roof
stone and one
course of cut
limestone

4 When you have built up to the level of the seat (about 430 mm – two courses of architectural stone and six of roof stone), fill the trough with topsoil, and place the stones for the arms of the seat.

5 Build the arms to 280 mm above the level of the seat (two courses of architectural stone and three of roof stone). Continue building the back to a total height of 870 mm above the ground.

Cleaning
Make a special job of cleaning
the top of the backrest

6 Finally, when the mortar is well cured, use a wire brush to clean all faces of the structure. Be careful not to blur the crisp finish of the mortar.

Cleaning
Make sure that
you clean the
mortar from
the faces of the
cut stone

Wire brushing
Use the brush
to define the
courses and
generally clean
up the stonework

Pedestal table

One of the joys of having a garden is being able to sit outside on a summer's evening and slowly sip a long, cool drink, relaxing in a comfortable chair. The picture is completed by the unique pedestal table that holds your drink.

TIME

Two weekends (eight hours to lay the foundation slab, eighteen hours to build the column, and a couple of hours to fit the flagstone).

SAFETY

The flagstone slab is incredibly heavy – it needs at least four strong, fit people to lift it.

YOU WILL NEED

Materials
for a table 900 mm square and 910 mm high
- Mortar: 2 parts (80 kg) cement, 1 part (40 kg) lime, 9 parts (360 kg) soft sand
- Concrete: 1 part (50 kg) cement, 2 parts (100 kg) sharp sand, 3 parts (150 kg) aggregate
- Slate or limestone flagstone for the table: about 900 mm square and 130 mm thick
- Flagstones for the plinth and capital: 2 stones about 570 mm square and 90 mm thick
- Split limestone: 1 cubic metre of salvaged roof stone, about 15 mm thick
- Hardcore: 0.5 cubic metres of rubble or broken stone

Tools
- Wheelbarrow
- Sack barrow
- Bucket
- Tape measure, straight-edge, piece of chalk
- Spade and shovel
- Sledgehammer
- Sawn wood: 4 lengths, about 660 mm long, 80 mm wide and 50 mm thick
- Wooden beam: about 600 mm long, 80 mm wide and 50 mm thick
- Mortar float
- Spirit level
- String and peg
- Bricklayer's trowel
- Mason's hammer
- Pointing trowel

ALL AROUND THE TABLE

In the context of this book, this project is monolithic. There is about one cubic metre of roof stone in the column, and the slab that goes to make the tabletop is so heavy that it takes four strong people to lift it into position. So you must start by assessing how you are going to shift the stone. For example, if you want the table at the end of the garden – over a bridge, the other side of the pond, and behind the border – it presents quite a challenge. You will have to ask family and neighbours to help. We used a wheelbarrow for the roof stone, and a sack barrow for the slabs.

The procedure for building the column is to select and shape pieces of roof stone to fit the circumference of the circle, set them in mortar, fill in the circle with more pieces of slate, and then move on to the next layer of mortar. Every few courses, rake out the mortar to reveal the slate, and make checks with the spirit level to ensure that the stones remain true.

CROSS-SECTION OF THE TABLE

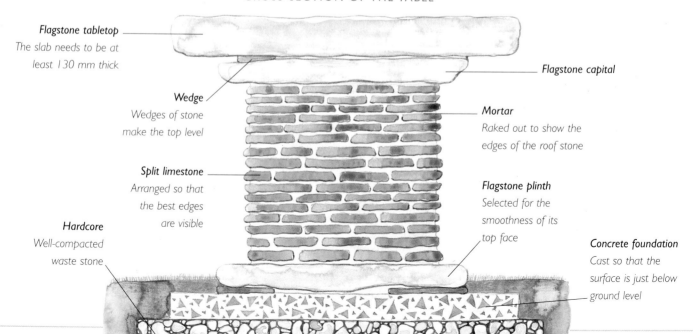

Flagstone tabletop
The slab needs to be at least 130 mm thick

Flagstone capital

Wedge
Wedges of stone make the top level

Mortar
Raked out to show the edges of the roof stone

Split limestone
Arranged so that the best edges are visible

Flagstone plinth
Selected for the smoothness of its top face

Hardcore
Well-compacted waste stone

Concrete foundation
Cast so that the surface is just below ground level

Pedestal table

FRONT VIEW OF THE TABLE

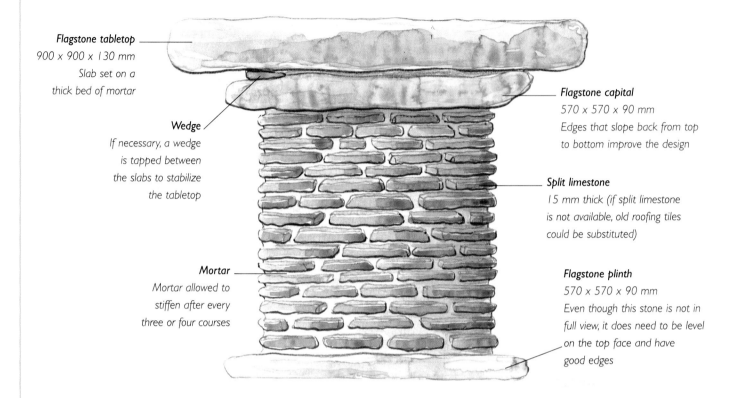

Flagstone tabletop
900 x 900 x 130 mm
Slab set on a
thick bed of mortar

Wedge
If necessary, a wedge
is tapped between
the slabs to stabilize
the tabletop

Mortar
Mortar allowed to
stiffen after every
three or four courses

Flagstone capital
570 x 570 x 90 mm
Edges that slope back from top
to bottom improve the design

Split limestone
15 mm thick (if split limestone
is not available, old roofing tiles
could be substituted)

Flagstone plinth
570 x 570 x 90 mm
Even though this stone is not in
full view, it does need to be level
on the top face and have
good edges

PLAN VIEW OF THE TABLE

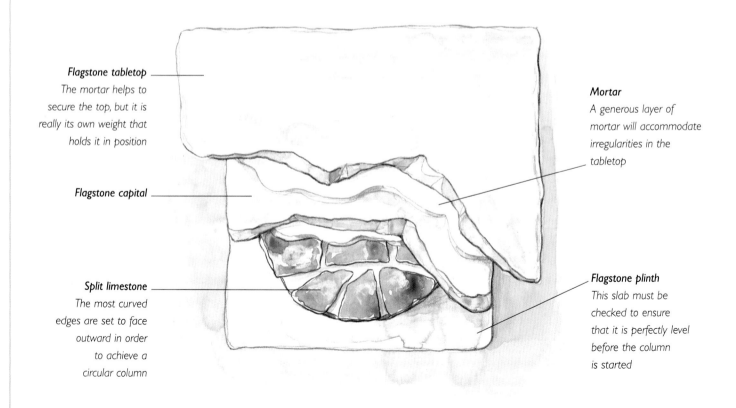

Flagstone tabletop
The mortar helps to
secure the top, but it is
really its own weight that
holds it in position

Flagstone capital

Split limestone
The most curved
edges are set to face
outward in order
to achieve a
circular column

Mortar
A generous layer of
mortar will accommodate
irregularities in the
tabletop

Flagstone plinth
This slab must be
checked to ensure
that it is perfectly level
before the column
is started

EXPLODED VIEW OF THE TABLE

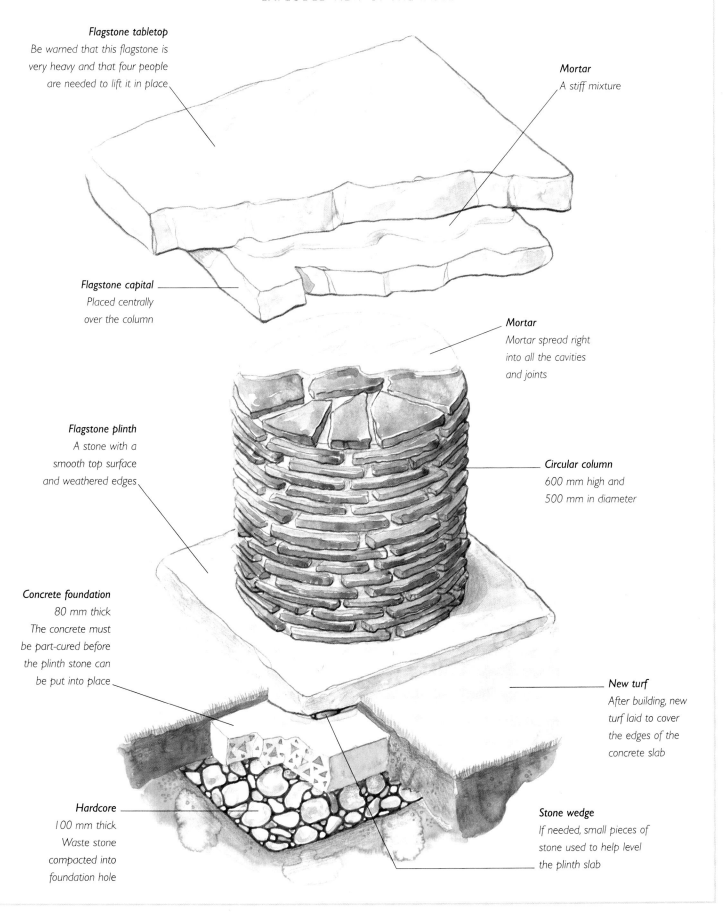

Flagstone tabletop
Be warned that this flagstone is
very heavy and that four people
are needed to lift it in place

Mortar
A stiff mixture

Flagstone capital
Placed centrally
over the column

Mortar
Mortar spread right
into all the cavities
and joints

Flagstone plinth
A stone with a
smooth top surface
and weathered edges

Circular column
600 mm high and
500 mm in diameter

Concrete foundation
80 mm thick
The concrete must
be part-cured before
the plinth stone can
be put into place

New turf
After building, new
turf laid to cover
the edges of the
concrete slab

Hardcore
100 mm thick
Waste stone
compacted into
foundation hole

Stone wedge
If needed, small pieces of
stone used to help level
the plinth slab

Step-by-step: Making the pedestal table

Floating
Float the concrete to a smooth finish

Split limestone
Pile up the stone so that it is close to hand

Frame
The frame measures 640 mm square

Levelling
Use the spirit level to check the slab is horizontal

Alignment
Position the plinth stone by using the chalked diagonals

1 Dig out the foundation to a depth of about 200 mm, making it 640 mm square, and half-fill it with hardcore. Ram it down with the sledgehammer. With the lengths of sawn wood, build a rough frame on the hardcore, measuring 640 mm square and 80 mm deep. Fill it up with concrete, and smooth it off with the wooden beam and mortar float.

2 When the concrete has set, remove the frame. Draw diagonals across the base slab to establish the centre, then set the plinth stone in place. Check that it is level with the spirit level. If it is not, insert slivers of stone until it lies horizontal.

Circle of stone
Bed the split stone in mortar to make a 500 mm-diameter circle

Levelling
Check the level after every five courses

Pointing
Pack the mortar under the edges of the plinth stone

Hammering
Tap individual stones to achieve an overall level surface

Trimming
Trim the edges of the stone for the best fit

3 Draw diagonals to establish the centre of the plinth stone, then draw a circle 500 mm in diameter using the string and peg. Use the bricklayer's trowel to butter the circle with mortar and place split limestone around the circumference.

4 Build up about five layers of limestone, then go round with the mason's hammer tapping individual stones into line. Make repeated checks with the spirit level. Continue building until the column is 600 mm high.

Adjusting
Tap proud stones
back into line

Bedding
Butter the top of the column
with a generous layer of mortar

Filling
Fill the
cavities with
mortar and
stone waste

Coursing
Rake out
the mortar to
reveal the
edges of
the stone

Column height
Aim for a
height of
600 mm

5 Walk around the column, checking that the sides are vertical, and use the mason's hammer to tap stones that are standing proud back into line.

6 Use the pointing trowel to butter the top of the finished column with a generous layer of mortar and carefully set the capital stone in place. Make sure that it is aligned with the plinth stone.

Mortar bedding
Butter the top of the capital
slab with a thick bed of mortar

7 Butter the capital slab with a thick layer of mortar, and then call on your helpers to lift the table slab into place. Check that it is level with the spirit level. If necessary, put slices of waste stone underneath to adjust the level until it lies horizontal.

Wedging
Use slices of
waste stone
underneath the
slab to maintain
the level

Helpful hint

Note the sack barrow in the background of this photo. If you intend doing heavy stone work – moving slabs or bags of cement, or even if you want to take some of the effort out of gardening, a traditional sack barrow is ideal.

Glossary

Backfilling To fill a hole around a foundation or wall with earth.

Bedding The process of pressing a stone into a bed or layer of wet mortar and ensuring that it is level.

Buttering The act of using a trowel to cover a piece of stone with wet mortar just prior to setting it in place on the bed of mortar.

Compacting Using a hammer or the weight of your body to press down a layer of sand, earth or hardcore.

Course A term describing the horizontal lines or layers of stone that make a wall or structure.

Coursing A general term describing the process of bedding a number of stones in mortar in order to build a course.

Curing time The time taken for mortar or concrete to become firm and stable. Part-cured mortar or concrete is firm enough to take a small amount of weight.

Damping Wetting the stone just prior to bedding in on mortar.

Dressing The act of using a hammer, chisel or trowel to trim a stone to a level, smooth, or textured finish.

Dry run See Trial run.

Floating The procedure of using a metal, plastic or wooden float to skim wet concrete or mortar to a smooth and completely level finish.

Levelling Using a spirit level to decide whether or not a structure or stone is level, and then making adjustments to bring individual stones into line.

Marking out Using a string, pegs and tape measure to set out the size of a foundation on the ground, also to mark out an individual stone in readiness for cutting to size.

Pointing Using a trowel, stick, or an alternative tool of your choice to bring the mortar joints to the desired finish.

Raking out Using a trowel to rake out part of the mortar, so that the edges of the stone are clearly revealed.

Sighting To judge by eye, or to look down or along a wall in order to determine whether or not the structure is level.

Siting Deciding whereabouts on the site – in the garden or on the plot – the structure is going to be placed.

Sourcing The process of finding out the best source for materials, at a price that you are happy with.

Tamping The act of using a length of wood to compact and level wet concrete.

Trial run Running through a procedure of setting out a structure without using concrete or mortar, in order to ascertain whether or not the envisaged project or technique is feasible.

Trimming Using a hammer, chisel or the edge of large trowel to bring the edge of a piece of stone to a good finish.

Wedging Using small slivers of stone to bring larger pieces up to the desired level.

Wire brushing The act of using a wire brush to remove dry mortar from the face of the stone.

Suppliers

UK

Consult the telephone directory for details of your local builder's yard or stone merchant.

The Brick Warehouse
18–22 Northdown Street
London N1 9BG
Tel: (020) 7833 9992

Buffalo Granite (UK) Ltd
The Vestry
St. Clement's Church
Treadgold Street
London W11 4BP
Tel: (020) 7221 7930

Clayax Yorkstone Ltd
Derry Hill
Menston
Ilkley
Leeds
West Yorkshire
LS29 6AZ
Tel: (01943) 878351
Fax: (01943) 870801

The Natural Stone Co
35 Bedford Road
Clapham
London SW4 7SG
Tel: (020) 7733 4455
Fax: (020) 7737 2427

Stonecraft
Burgh Road
Aylsham
NR11 6AR
Tel: (020) 8242 9017 ext. 25

**General DIY Outlets
(branches nationwide)**

B & Q plc
Head Office:
Portswood House
1 Hampshire Corporate Park
Chandlers Ford
Eastleigh, Hants
SO53 3YX
Tel: (01703) 256256

Focus Do-It-All Group Ltd
Head Office:
Gawsworth House
Westmere Drive
Crewe
Cheshire
CW1 6XB
Tel: (01384) 456456

Homebase Ltd
Beddington House
Railway Approach
Wallington
Surrey
SM6 0HB
Tel: (020) 8784 7200

SOUTH AFRICA

*Consult your telephone directory
for your local branch of Mica
Hardware or Federated Timbers.*

Dunrobin Garden Pavilion
Old Main Road
Bothas Hill, Durban
Tel: (031) 777 1855
Fax: (031) 777 1893

Lifestyle Garden Centre
DF Malan Drive
Randpark Ridge
Northcliff, Johannesburg
Tel: (011) 792 5616
Fax: (011) 792 5332

Radermachers Garden &
    Home Centre
Kraaibosch, National Road
George
Tel: (044) 889 0075/6
Fax: (044) 889 0071

Safari Garden Centre
Lynwood Road
Pretoria
Tel: (012) 807 0009
Fax: (012) 807 0350

Showgrounds Nursery
Showgrounds
Currie Avenue
Bloemfontein
Tel: (051) 447 5523
Fax: (051) 447 5523

Starke Ayres
322 Kempston Road
Sydwill, Port Elizabeth
Tel: (041) 451 0389
Fax: (041) 451 0393

Stodels
Eversdal Road
Bellville, Cape Town
Tel: (021) 99 1106
Fax: (021) 919 9324

Stoneage Concrete
    Industries cc
126 Crompton Street
Pinetown, Durban
Tel: (031) 701 2411
Fax: (031) 701 6842

AUSTRALIA

General building equipment

ABC Timbers and Building
    Supplies Pty Ltd
46 Auburn Road
Regents Park NSW 2143
Tel: (02) 9645 2511

BBC Hardware
Building A
Cnr. Cambridge &
    Chester Streets
Epping
NSW 2121
Tel: (02) 9876 0888
(Branches throughout Australia)

BBC Hardware
Niangala Close
Belrose NSW 2085
Tel: (02) 9450 0799
(Can also order in stone)

Bowens Timber and
    Building Supplies
135–173 Macaulay Road
North Melbourne 3051
Tel: (03) 9328 1041

Mitre 10
319 George Street
Sydney 2000
Tel: (02) 9262 1435
Customer service: 1800 777 850
Outlets nationwide including:
Greens Hardware
cnr Maryvale and Peel Street
South Brisbane
Queensland 4101
Tel: (07) 3844 3341

Cleveland Mitre 10
25–31 Shore Street West
Cleveland
Queensland 4163
Tel: (07) 3821 1153

Stone suppliers

Kellyville Landscape Supplies
Lot 25
Windsor Road
Kellyville NSW 2155
Tel: (02) 9629 4167

Sydney Stone Yard
1/3a Stanley Road
Randwick NSW 2031
Tel: (02) 9326 4479

NEW ZEALAND

Firth Industries Limited
Auckland Regional Office
102 Lunn Ave
Mt Wellington
Auckland
Information Freephone:
    0800 800 576
(Branches nationwide)

Mitre 10
Head Office:
182 Wairau Road
Glenfield
Auckland
Tel: (09) 443 9900
(Branches nationwide)

Placemakers Support Office
150 Marua Road
Private Bag 14942
Panmure
Auckland
Tel: (09) 525 5100

Conversion chart

To convert the metric measurements given in this book to imperial measurements, simply multiply the figure given in the text by the relevant number shown in the table below. Bear in mind that conversions will not necessarily work out exactly, and you will need to round the figure up or down slightly. (Do not use a combination of metric and imperial measurements — for accuracy, keep to one system.)

To convert	Multiply by
millimetres to inches	0.0394
metres to feet	3.28
metres to yards	1.093
sq millimetres to sq inches	0.00155
sq metres to sq feet	10.76
sq metres to sq yards	1.195
cu metres to cu feet	35.31
cu metres to cu yards	1.308
grams to pounds	0.0022
kilograms to pounds	2.2046
litres to gallons	0.22

Index

Acknowledgments

The authors are grateful to Ian Parsons (photographer) for helping to lift the heaviest stones.

AG&G Books would like to thank the following picture libraries for their contribution: *Dennis Davis Photography Design* (pages 68, 94 top and 94 bottom); *Garden and Wildlife Matters* (pages 46 bottom and 69 inset) and *John Glover Photography* (page 46 top).